JETTI HARRIS IS A CHII  us
wonder about the mystery c ve
for us in Jesus Christ. Her r /i-
tation to live before God's face by joining the music which the stars
sang together at the dawn of creation.

John D. Witvliet
Calvin Institute of Christian Worship

THE BEST AUTHORS ARE THOSE who do two things together.
First, they specialize, and Jetti is a specialist in music (theory and ap-
plication). Second, they lustfully explore secondary areas, even ones
that at first glance do not overlap. And as they explore these secondary
areas, they open the curtains to reveal interweavings that no audience
has yet appreciated and no ambassador has yet proclaimed. Jetti is
such an author and herald. Prepare to put glasses on that will show you
music in, literally, a new light. Such that your old view of music will
seem trite, pedestrian, and well, small.

Ronald L. Giese, Jr., Ph.D.
Pastor of Leadership Development
Desert Springs Church
Albuquerque, New Mexico

IN AN AGE WHEN MUSIC PROGRAMS ARE BEING CUT in
schools from one end of the country to the other, Jetti Harris is a won-
derfully poignant example of how teaching classical music to students
at an early age gives those students a more worldly outlook for the rest
of their lives.

Paul Plishka
Bass, Metropolitan Opera

October 25, 2011

For Sarah,

May God's song ring out
you in joy, always be your
strength and hope. Thank you for just being
you! Love,
Jetti

"...He will rejoice over you with great gladness. With his love, he will calm all your fears. He will exult over you by singing a happy song."

— **Zephaniah 3:17,** *NLT*

God's Song

FINDING TRUTH IN MUSIC

JETTI HARRIS

LIBERTY
UNIVERSITY.
Press

God's Song
by Jetti Harris

ISBN-13: 978-1-935986-04-1

Cover & Interior Design:

Megan Johnson
Johnson2Design
Johnson2Design.com

LIBERTY UNIVERSITY™ Press

Lynchburg, VA

Table of Contents

Part 1: Exposition

Table of Contents

Table of Contents

Table of Contents

Preface

THE STORY BEHIND THE BOOK, *GOD'S SONG*

The "story behind the story" may be just as compelling as the story itself. I suspect this to be the case with God's Song. At least, there are things that must be attended to in order to make this work complete. There are people to be thanked, friends to be recognized and feelings and shared emotions to be explored, analyzed and accepted.

As Jana, my alter-ego or pseudo-name, the world I lived in was certainly not a sterile world. It reflected color and love, hope and despair, song and dirge and always, flights of fantasy which resulted in inquisitive thinking that propelled me like a jet engine on an airplane. I guess my mother prophetically named me "Jettie" or "Jetti" or "Jetty"—they all have the same connotation. The diminutive form is, nonetheless, "Jet."

The path has been difficult. It is very hard to live with one who is always in motion—as Jana or Jetti—always was—and probably still is. Old age does not change the mind-set. Be advised.

I shall attempt to take the issues at hand in some sort of order dictated by the difficulty with which they can be addressed. Gratitude should be a basic

human response and should, therefore, also be the most important thing with which to deal.

Every single person whose life crossed mine at any given point needs to be acknowledged with deep gratitude. There are many whose names did not make it into the book, simply because there was not time or space in a work like this to give pages to so many who were really so important. I think of one whom I should name, Lois-Ellin Greene, a fellow-student at Fairmont West Side High School. She wrote a poem about me that I have long since, to my own distress, lost, and she was a great companion who knew me well and could always see through the mist into the real heart of things.

There were teachers who put up with the precocious brat who refused to be tamed and could find more answers to fewer questions than could be asked. There were cousins who gave me a battering ram against which to brace my driving will. My parents put up with loud talk and argument with a bright child they did not always understand. They always did their very best for me.

My deepest thanks to my brother and sister who never knew how in the world to relate to their unruly sister. I love them both very deeply.

Then, there is my beloved son, Kenneth, who has, through all of this journey of discovery in the last ten years, been my intellectual partner. An un-degreed engineer himself, he has been in close company with men in high intellectual places and held his own and has, therefore, been of great encouragement to me when I felt completely overwhelmed. And, with his great ability to understand, he has been a continual source of inspiration and scholarly challenge to me. Ideas are his forte.

There are those who can be named—like my daughter, Gail, who had a vision of her mom's real persona and stood by it and always prayed for

me. Then, there are those who are absent because of other very sad realities. And, oh, how I have longed to be able to share these imminently triumphant moments of seeing this work reach fruition with my middle-button daughter, Nancy.

Another group of people whom I do not know how to thank are the great thinkers and writers of our time whom I have been privileged to become acquainted with through my own research and study. May I name some of them at the risk of leaving some un-named?

Ron Giese taught me Hebrew so I could do my own research in the scriptures. Jeremy Begbie taught me the great lesson of continuing to seek *truth in music* because it IS inherent. Nicholas Woltersdorff, Don Wilson, Quentin Faulkner, John Witvliet, Tom Schwanda, Eckhardt Schnabel, Andrew Sauerwein, and many others. These people encouraged me to keep thinking and keep writing until I could satisfy my own soul that I had done my best and was ready to share with the world what I have learned.

A very special thanks must be expressed to the two people who saw "Jana" through the last few weeks of the editing process—Father Christopher Heying of St. Stephen's Episcopal Church, Forest, Va., and Sandra Thompson, from Saint Andrew Presbyterian Church, Lynchburg, Va. These two people gave selflessly and devotedly in making the last edit of the book a reality.

And then, there are the great loves of my life. For a child of ten or fifteen or seventy-eight, it is of utmost importance to experience the great loves in life in order to be able to express the swirling emotions which are inherent to this book. And, yes, Jana loved deeply and she loved well and she, in a certain sense, has not abandoned her deep loves just because life has taken her into another dimension. Her first great love, was, of course, her love for her heavenly Father and Lord. But in order

to understand the intricacies and depths of that love, God Himself gave us the element of human love as an example. Hence, the welter of great people who crossed Jana's path as she journeyed through life: Robert Dvorak, Paul Schocker, Walt Rybeck and Thelma Loudin. These were people who facilitated her first tangible connection with love which transcends and who gave her the curiosity to explore love that can and *does* heal. Her experience with the music of Brahms as a dying child of ten had reinforcement in the experiences of love that she experienced later in the person of her friends and teachers. God gives us such people if we are sensitive enough to look for them.

And then, there is the ultimate person to be thanked—my beloved husband and companion of twenty-three years.

We were such an "odd couple." One of EJ's closest friends once said, "It sure is funny—you two together—very funny."

EJ, the pragmatic pilot and engineer. "Jana," the frazzled, emotional musician, tempered only by her own determination to master reason by learning to fly—and, yet, the "odd couple" became the "perfect couple," whose love could never be questioned.

These last ten years, EJ has seen "Jana" through all kinds of cycles of hope, exhilaration, denial, loss of faith, despair and finally, triumphant completion.

Last of all, the great team of people who made this book possible—Liberty University Press—must be thanked. Most of them are very young and must be wished well on their own journey of discovery. God bless you, one and all.

It has been a wonderful, frightening and satisfying journey.

Preface

Before closing this preface, I must make the most important acknowledgement of all and that is to my Lord and Creator, who called me to this incredible task of dispersing His message to all who will hear. Praise to You, Lord God.

Part 1
EXPOSITION

Chapter 1

THEME ONE: MOTIF I: MUSIC: ATTACA

The walls in the tiny bedroom were odd. They were a kind of buttery yellow cream color and dappled, like sun through the leaves of a huge tree, with a kind of repulsive thick blue color. There was no pattern. A kind of new place to live emerged out of that glut of ugly color. It wasn't a pretty place—just a maze of small, thick blue splashes which made little roads to walk on and bushes to hide behind and little trees to curl up under. The buttery yellow background was soft though, and cooling to look at. The little girl who lay there in the hot sweaty fold of her bed knew somehow that she was very, very sick and, maybe, if she could find one of those imaginary blue trees to sit under, she might begin to get better.

Her mother came into the room with their town's old-maid physician, Dr. Flood. Somehow the name fitted her. When she came into the room there didn't seem to be any air left there to breathe. And the little girl needed air—lots of it—because she was very hot. And very frightened. Her mother looked apprehensively at Dr. Flood and asked, "Is she going to be okay?"

Dr. Flood looked grim, with her hair knotted tightly at the back of her neck. "I am afraid she is very ill. We've had a lot of scarlet fever this spring and two of the kids haven't made it. But we will do everything that we can and we'll see…"

She turned on her heel and left. The mother came over and felt the little girl's head. Hot! Hot and dry, and her breath smelled of sickness. She smoothed a cold, wet cloth on her child's forehead as she began to drift off to sleep.

A bit later, the little girl—let's call her Jana—drifted back into wakefulness. She stared at the wall, imagining that she was walking all alone on a creamy road between two blue trees, when she heard the most beautiful music. Her daddy had brought a small radio for her, and since she was too delirious to care which station to listen to, he had tuned it to WJZ in New York. The room suddenly came alive with the sound of a violin and piano. Slow low-throated chords on the piano felt like the slow steps Jana was trying to take up the fantasy hill on her painted bedroom wall— slow and painful. Then the violin began to sing wondrously, down low in its range and climbing inexorably up and up the melodic and harmonic ladder, out of darkness and ever upward until it emerged in a glorious wash of beauty, like suddenly catching a glimpse of what lay beyond.

"Mother, what was that music?" she called loudly, as a cooling chill ran through her fever-ridden body. "What was it?"

Her mother sat on the edge of her bed. Before she could answer, the announcer said, "Listen again tomorrow at five fifteen for the next installment of *The Guiding Light*."

It was 1942. *The Guiding Light* was a radio drama of Old Testament stories. What mattered to Jana was that the theme song played

4

for a minute or two at the start and end of each episode. The announcer naturally did not say what the music was. Jana just knew that she had to live another day to hear it again. So it went for more than a week, living from day to day to hear that glorious music again. Each day brought her nearer to a day when the fever finally broke and Dr. Flood stated rather impersonally that Jana would recover. Nothing was said about the role of the music.

This seemingly miraculous experience is a true story. That radio theme was the opening call of a long voyage down the halls of music. Interestingly, the cooling chill that ran through Jana's body that day as a harbinger of recovery was not a one-time event. That same health-giving chill runs through her being, both physically and spiritually, whenever she hears music that conveys some truth or deep feeling. Jana learned to trust this reaction to beauty. Her story is an exploration of the mystery of music—a life-long quest to fathom what is, at its essential core, this thing we call music.

For months after Jana recovered from scarlet fever, the memory of the fragment of music to which she had clung so desperately haunted her. She tried to pick it out on the piano, tried to tell her piano teacher at the Catholic school about it, tried to recall the pitches so she could hum it. All to no avail. That music was lost for the next fifty or sixty years, until…

But that can wait.

Chapter 2

SFORZANDO: WAR TIME AT WEST POINT

orld War II was raging, changing the course of everyone's lives. Jana reaped a reward from these changes. She lived at Highland Falls near the Military Academy at West Point. Many musicians who had not qualified for combat for one reason or another ended up in military bands, providing music for the troops and for those who taught the troops. Some of the best of those came to West Point.

It was an exciting windfall for a girl of ten. She loved the regular Sunday afternoon concerts at the gymnasium on the Reservation, as the grounds of West Point were called. One had to have a pass to get on the Reservation. Jana supposed this was to keep out traitors who would do harm of some kind. So she valued her pass as a special gift from her piano teacher, Robert J. Dvorak, who played French horn in the Army band.

Robert was twenty-three at the time, and married to a beautiful coloratura soprano. He had been playing in the Chicago Symphony before the war brought him to West Point. He also became organist in nearby Highland Falls at the small Methodist church Jana's family attended. On Sundays,

Jana sat with her little brother at the back of the church waiting for the choir to process into the sanctuary. Robert would already be at the organ, ready to play the prelude. She was always enchanted watching Robert. He usually wore his dress blues for Sunday services, and oh, how tall, handsome and elegant he was. The dark blue jacket fitted him so closely, making his shoulders look even wider than they were. There was a red satin braid around the high collar and shoulder epaulets and polished gold buttons all down the front. Jana mused as she watched him setting the stops on the organ: "He makes the sound of the music look as beautiful as it sounds. I wonder why color and music are so much alike? And I wonder what this feeling deep inside of my brain is and why I love beauty so much?"

One particular morning was special as he started to play softly with a purity and romance which stirred Jana's mind to wandering again. She had no idea where this enchantment came from or why beautiful music could so completely transport her from mundane thoughts to a fantasy world. As she sat in the back pew mesmerized by Robert's playing, she experienced a soaring of her childish spirit that took her to a place of calm and peace, far from the raucousness of her daily life. She could hardly wait for the end of a long dry sermon so she could run up and talk to the organist.

After Dvorak released the last chord of the postlude, she walked up into the choir loft and blurted out, "Hello! I want you to teach me the piece you played before church. I play the piano, sort of, and I know I can learn to play the organ, too."

"Well, young lady, do you think you can reach the organ pedals? I'm glad you liked the piece—it was the Berceuse from an opera called *Jocelyn*. It calls for playing the pedals."

"If I can't reach them, I'll exercise hard so I'll get taller. I'm sure I can. Will you teach me?"

Could Jana reach the pedals? Or did Sgt. Dvorak suggest she start with piano lessons first? Probably the latter, though time has blurred the answer. But the memory of being able to sit and play with this wonderful musician has not blurred. The lessons, whether piano or organ, were three dollars an hour and, oh, what a marvelous hour that was every week. Eventually she learned that Berceuse on both the piano and the organ.

Jana could not seem to get her fill of music. Every Sunday afternoon during the winter months she walked four miles to the West Point gym to see and hear the huge and excellent Army band. It did not matter to her that clarinets played the violin parts or that the tuba substituted for the double string bass. These arrangements gave Jana her first glimpses of some of the most beautiful compositions ever written.

One day at her lesson, Robert said to Jana, "Be sure to be at the band concert next Sunday. There will be a special soloist there to play Edvard Grieg's A minor Piano Concerto with the band. His name is Percy Grainger."

"Who is he?" Classical music and musicians were strangers to Jana's home life, although her family came from a long line of Appalachian mountain musicians. Her grandfather and most of her uncles and aunts could not read a note of music, yet remarkably, they could play all kinds of instruments from the piano to the banjo. "I never heard of Percy Grainger."

"Well, he's one of the finest composers and pianists of this century. He's from Australia and now lives in America. It's very special that we can hear him at West Point. I'll get you a seat near the front so you can see and hear everything."

When Grainger walked onto the stage, Jana was astounded at the great shock of wild curly white hair that dominated his figure—like a great stick of white cotton candy. Her amazement at his appearance was nothing compared to her amazement at his performance. He sat on the bench, adjusted his coattails and gently caressed the keyboard. There was a quiet hush as he poised his hands above the keys. Then came a tremendous rush of crashing melody as he pounced on the upper octaves of the piano—taaa, ta ta taa, ta ta taa, ta ta taa, tatatatata—as the orchestra joined in the great morass of sound. Jana felt those same chills as when she was so ill and had lived for the music. More than the music, she sensed instinctively that music was a vehicle for something greater, but the little girl was unable to form into words what she was feeling.

Chapter 3

MOTIF II: MUSIC: CANTABILE

As time passed and the intensified war eclipsed other concerns, uncles and family friends went off to fight. The music at least was still there, as was Robert. He introduced her to the wonders of Russian program music, presenting her with an album of *Pictures at an Exhibition* by Rimsky-Korsakoff, and then transporting himself into the characters of the composition: the Ba-Ba-Ya-Ga, the witch on the clock; Schmeel, the argumentative Jew; and the battling chicks in the barnyard. Jana remembered giggling uncontrollably as Robert hopped around the kitchen table with his legs bent way down and his arms and hands contorted into ugly demonic-looking shapes and cackling like a witch. Then he suddenly stood up and, with great flailing motions, made intimidating gestures as he argued with the imaginary Jewish opponent on the other side of the table. As quickly as he had transformed himself from witch to angry Jew, he became not one, but two, screeching chicks, screaming and flying wickedly at each other from one kitchen chair to another. All this in his tiny kitchen, with his wife Lola laughing indulgently. For all of his charades, Robert made Jana

feel grown up as he talked to her about musical themes, life and death, and the meanings of Easter.

Soon it was Easter of 1945 and Jana was thirteen. Thursdays after school she walked the five miles to the enlisted men's chapel on the north side of the post for choir rehearsal. After the long walk, the thrill of singing in a grown-up choir took the little girl into another world for almost two whole hours.

Robert had written a beautiful cantata celebrating Eastertide and Jana was the only child in the choir. Everyone else, trained and adult, seemed happy to have precocious Jana in their midst. The cantata—the horrors of the crucifixion, the sorrow of loss and the ultimate resurrection—was almost more than she could take in. Yet somehow the music sustained her and she reveled in being part of it. She later recalled sensing that the music itself, aside from the Easter story, had its own tale to tell, a tale that she could not quite fathom.

Little did Jana know that Robert's composition would become a veritable emotional companion to her that would sustain her through heavy personal difficulties. Music, she found, could do that.

Chapter 4

LARGHETTO: RITARDANDO AND ACCELERANDO

*L*ife was so fulfilling for three years that Jana's first real disappointments were a big blow.

Robert and Lola were leaving. He had won a full-time contract with the
Chicago Symphony—a piece of good fortune for him. For Jana, though, it
was the sad ending of an era. Not only that, Robert had worked out a plan to
enroll Jana in the preparatory school at the Curtis Institute of Music in Phila-
delphia to advance her budding piano studies in the best available way. But
her parents, unschooled in the world of the performing arts, recoiled from
having their child "let loose in the big city." No amount of reassurance that
their girl would receive proper and loving care satisfied them. Their response
to the plan was an emphatic and irrevocable "No!"

Just before the Dvoraks left their little Highland Falls house on Lake
Street, Robert did two things to ease Jana's distress.

First, he introduced his young student to *Death and Transfiguration* by
Richard Strauss. The great German composer's tone poem depicted a dying

man (a friend of Strauss, according to legend) and his agonizing struggle to find release from the pangs of his imminent demise. The music tells the story in more graphic and poignant fashion than any word could: the rhythms of the percussion coupled with the death-dance sounds of the string section portray the approaching death angel. The agony of breathless laboring against that angel is inescapable. Then comes a moment of sudden stillness. The man is released from his struggle. He sees the light of inner salvation and succumbs to the vision of a beautiful place to which he will soon be transported. The music ascends to a place of incredible light and peace and the transfiguration is completed. Rest at last.

Jana was ecstatic. She did not want to return to the monotony and discordant harshness of her daily routine. She had discovered that peace and healing existed, but she could find them nowhere except in music.

After giving Jana one last piano lesson, Robert announced his second surprise: "Jana, I have a new teacher for you." As she sighed with relief at not having to return to the mediocre teacher she had before Robert, at the convent school, he continued. "A very dear friend in the band plays the harp, the flute, and the piano. I've spoken to him and he is anxious to meet you and be your teacher. His name is Paul Schocker."

Chapter 5

ACCELERANDO: A NEW STAR AND A HEAVENLY SHOW

And so it was. A week later came a knock on the door at 51 Schneider Avenue where Jana lived. It was early spring but still bitterly cold. There, in a long Army drab overcoat, stood a man so tall Jana could not see his face without tilting up her head. To her he was so handsome she was mesmerized. His eyes twinkled and his mouth curved into a playful smile.

"I'm Paul. And you must be Jana."

Being only thirteen, feeling awkward and ugly, and taken aback, all she could say was, "Mother, come quick, someone's here."

In their first weeks of getting acquainted, the start of a deep and meaningful relationship, Jana poured all of the feelings stirring inside her into her music. Her first assignment was Rachmaninoff's Prelude in C# Minor, and how she struggled with it. The huge black key octaves, all filled in with notes, made her hands feel like they were turning upside down and getting criss-crossed. A whirlwind let loose on the second page careened up the

keyboard until fire bells clanged and horses' hooves pounded back down the keyboard, only to burst into the most liberating sounds of triumphant conquest a piano could possibly make.

Paul told her a beguiling story about the piece: "The 1917 Russian revolution brought terrible hardship and many died. Rachmaninoff lived in Moscow and reportedly was hiding in the catacombs of a cathedral when heard up above the clanging of fire bells and the pounding hooves of the fire wagon's horses, and that was his inspiration for this Prelude." Jana never knew, or cared, if the story was true. It fit her musical fantasies perfectly, especially since her teacher was seventeen months old when his parents fled with him from Russia to America.

In 1944 and 1945 life was filled with concerts at West Point, two or three choir rehearsals a week, and of course piano lessons. Jana also began to play the organ in her little Highland Falls Methodist Church when the choir director could not come because of Army duties. Arthur Christmann, a well-known New York City clarinetist, had become organist after Robert left. Christmann's busy schedule gave Jana lots of practice serving in his place.

One unforgettably rare evening Jana was walking down the big hill on Schneider Avenue to the church. It was cold and getting dark. Suddenly the whole atmosphere seemed to come alive. For no apparent reason, there was an electric excitement in the air. Then she saw it—a spear of red-green-blue light that came out of the north sky and shot across the azimuth. It wouldn't stay still. It shimmered and undulated and danced and changed shapes quicker than the eye could follow. Then, it started taking the shape of a huge pointed dome right over her head and turned brilliant red and green, making Jana feel as if she were inside an incredible heavenly cathedral with a dome so high it reached into eternity. She

was frozen in her tracks, staring up into the Technicolor night and vibrating inside in tune with those glorious dancing colors.

Suddenly she headed to the parsonage, running until her breath was all but gone, bounding up the porch steps and pounding on the door.

"Mrs. Venable, come quick! You have to see what I just saw. Look."

By then, sadly, the glory she had witnessed was spent and the sky merely twinkled with the light of a thousand stars. Jana never overcame the thrill of that first encounter with the aurora borealis. For years and even decades, she waited eagerly as fall advanced into winter in the hope of being enveloped just once more in that unbelievable cosmic spectacle.

Often, sitting by the bank of a pond in a park near her home, Jana wondered what that heavenly display would sound like if it could sing. Little did she suspect then that she would later find indications that the aurora, in its way, does sing a song—a song of ethereal beauty beyond imagination.

Chapter 6

Maestoso: A Majestic Instrument

Things of magnificent proportions intrigued Jana. The organ in the West Point Cadet Chapel, like the aurora borealis, was one of those things. She would muse about the organ's powerful attraction as she climbed the hill to the huge castle-like Gothic cathedral that dominated the entire landscape above the parade grounds and the Hudson River. She marveled about her enviable position of having not only a brilliant piano teacher, but also a fine organ teacher, Frederick C. Mayer. Slightly built with white hair, Frederick and the chapel's new organ had both arrived at West Point in 1911. And now, years later in the '40s, Jana was privileged to be his student.

As one of his favored students, Jana loved her lesson times with Frederick and with the organ. She loved the echoing thud of her footsteps on granite floors as she walked down the aisle to the organ console. An organist had to go down a few steps to the bench and then look up at the row after row of stops and couplers. To Jana it was like being wrapped in a protective womb where no harm could come to her. She regretted the end of her lessons when

she had to face reality—her ailing father, her unhappy mother, and her quarrelsome siblings.

On that glorious instrument she even enjoyed her finger substitution exercises—the technique of keeping organ tones sustained and singing instead of sounding staccato. Frederick was understanding when she had not bothered to practice on that "dumb little organ," as she called it, in the Methodist church. She felt it was unfair to be shackled to that pitiful instrument, complaining to herself so much that it stood in the way of learning as much as she should have.

When her father's illness forced the family to leave Highland Falls, Jana would miss most of all the Chapel organ and Frederick. She could not imagine then that fate would give her a chance, years later, to reprise this phase of her life and again play that awe-inspiring instrument under Frederick's loving tutelage for a time.

Jana's love of the pipe organ was burnt deep in her soul. To understand the organ's power and ethos became, after her Chapel days, a part of her increasingly insistent quest to unravel the mysteries of music.

Chapter 7

A CAPELLA: TAKING ON A NEW ROLE

oung Jana by the mid-1940s had grown into a mature pre-teen in many ways, although in other ways she was the epitome of child-ish exuberance and frenetic activity. Her mind was always on the fly, often to places her peers could not begin to understand. Like the time the Chapman girls and Bobbie came to pick her up for Sunday evening church.

"Come on," Etta said, "we'll be late if you don't turn off that radio and get going." Etta was four years older than Jana but in the same class at school because, unlike precocious Jana, Etta was slow and more interested in Army boys than studies.

"All you care about is going to youth group to see who you can pick up," Jana snapped at her. "You have no idea how beautiful this music is, and that it has to be heard to the very end to see how it is going to settle itself. This is Caesar Franck's Symphony in D Minor, all about the sadness of life, but none of you really care. You all go on and I'll get there when I get there."

Jana had this way of making her friends uncomfortable and she was often left alone. When the three young people left her house, Jana's mother was

pretty sharp with her: "You don't know how to treat your friends. It's a wonder they ever come around."

Crying, Jana ran out of the house and headed for the church, but she had other things on her mind. Paul had given her his last piano lesson because he was getting out of the Army and going back to Easton, Pennsylvania. It was the fall of 1945. The war ended that summer. Robert was gone. Now Paul was gone. Most of the young musicians Jana knew in the Army band were gone, too. Because Robert had left, she no longer sang in the Enlisted Men's Chapel Choir. Because Arthur Christmann also had left, she had become church organist. Life had become painfully lonely and the days hung heavy and sad for Jana.

She was thirteen when her principal at the public school called her into his office. Mr. O'Neill was a tall thin man with a compact black mustache and thinning black hair. He greeted Jana and asked her to sit down. What he had to say stunned her: "Several mothers have been coming in to see me. They can't find piano teachers for their kids because so many men from the Army band left. We know how hard you have been working on your music and we wondered: would you be willing to take a few students?"

Actually, before Paul Schocker left, he suggested Jana look into taking on students after the war ended, but she had not given it further thought. In small Highland Falls, with maybe four or five thousand people, one of the few places to find a music teacher was the Ladycliff Academy School for girls. The director of a community chorus and his daughter also taught, but they couldn't handle many students.

How does a youngster react to being asked to take over the students of fine teachers whom she admired almost reverently? Hers was not an easy decision to think through and there weren't many people she could

talk to about it. Her parents, of course, were proud Jana was asked to take on this responsibility, but they felt it made no sense. Teaching serious music was no childish occupation and, to them, Jana was still a child. The more they made this point, the more she was convinced otherwise. If Paul and Mr. O'Neill thought she could teach, she finally determined she would do it. And so she did.

A couple years later she was walking home from teaching a lesson on Lake Street, the very street where she used to take her own lessons. Curiously, when she reached Main Street, there at the bus stop was Paul Schocker. He had come to West Point on Army business and was taking the bus to New York City where he would catch a train back to Easton. Jana was so excited she ran full speed across the street and threw herself into his arms. Practically a woman now at fifteen, with puzzling stirrings inside her, she felt in love with this handsome man who knew so much that she had to learn and who, she believed, was the only one who could open up new musical vistas for her.

Paul gave her a fatherly smile and said he was glad they had bumped into each other because he had a present for her. He stooped his great height down, laid his briefcase on the ground, opened it, took out a yellow Schirmer score book and handed it to Jana. She read in big black letters: **J. S. Bach**, and beneath that, **CHACONNE IN D MINOR.**

"This is a very difficult work, Jana. It will take a long time to learn, but you must master it. It will improve your technique. More than that, it will make your musicianship grow fast. Once you understand this work, it will make you a mature artist." Quite a challenge.

By July of 1947, ready to be a high school senior at fifteen, Jana was a year ahead of the norm. Thanks to Paul and to her busy schedule of teaching, which had become her great love, she had enjoyed several good

and rewarding years. There was even talk of a full scholarship for her at a New York university. Yet her mind was not at ease.

Troubling questions continued to build within her. What is music, after all? Why does music make me feel things I can't begin to describe? Why does the world of nature intrigue and move me so intensely? What really happened that night when I saw the aurora? Why is music called the universal language? And isn't it more than language—but what?

Chapter 8

INTERLUDE: A LOOK BACK

To take stock of who Jana was becoming merits a pause for reflection.

How often she relived the time when a piece of music literally spared her, as she was totally convinced, from the jaws of death. Incidentally, she still had not identified the composition. Following that intervention, she thought the two most momentous events to come her way were meeting her two exceptional teachers. They shaped her life emotionally and intellectually as they helped give voice to her own talents.

Young Robert Dvorak was just the right person to take a child who had not been exposed to the vastness and beauties of the musical world and lead her, musically speaking, into the land of Narnia. He was an inspiring mentor, able to translate her own vague feelings into sounds that could be created, listened to and thought about. He gave her the first opportunities to express the questioning in her soul by allowing her to sing in the West Point choir and by introducing her to the realm of gracious pianistic performance.

Next came Paul Schocker, who happened to be the first-born of an Orthodox Jewish family. She loved him as a young girl does, and her adoration lasted, sustaining her later when life seemed to suck the very air out of her lungs. When she needed but could not find love and beauty, Paul's name became a comforting mantra for her. More than that, she felt Paul's greatest gift to her was sharing his deep spiritual understanding, a sense of God's presence in the beauties of the world. He brought this perspective to music, revealed in the structure and ineffable qualities of the rhythmic and harmonic configurations with which musicians deal on a daily basis. He transmitted to Jana his captivating sensitivity to what made beautiful music possible. If this sounds unsubstantial or ethereal, Paul nevertheless was a master at teaching the critical elements of music theory which evade most young aspiring musicians.

Those precious years with Robert and Paul equipped Jana well for her circuitous journey that was to follow.

Chapter 9

AGITATO: DISRUPTING CHANGES

Time seemed to accelerate for Jana in the summer between her junior and senior high school years. Daddy complained incessantly that he felt bad. Mother had to get up at 5:30 to arrive by 7:00 at the tailor shop in West Point where her work was hard. Jana's friend and Highland Falls High School music teacher, Carolyn Kyle, was leaving for a better job. Jana's boyfriend Ross moved to California. She was lonely and everything had turned to dissonance. Then worse happened.

On a Sunday night Jana and her family were supposed to go to Croton-on-Hudson for a farewell party and concert for Carolyn Kyle. It also happened to be July 6, 1947, daddy and mother's 21st wedding anniversary. On that fateful day, Jana's father had a massive heart attack. Dr. Flood, grim as ever, came and her diagnosis was not good. Daddy was confined indefinitely to bed.

By late August arrangements had been made to move the entire family to West Virginia to live with Aunt Rose who owned a restaurant and board-

ing house in Fairmont. Aunt Rose, mother's older sister, was formidable. She glowered when she talked. A Brunhilde type, she stomped when she walked.

The pending move was a crushing blow to Jana. She had been offered a chance for a full scholarship at Pottsdam State Music College, assuming she completed her senior year and obtained a New York State Regents diploma from high school.

"Mother, please," she said, begging to stay behind. "Aunt Maude said I could stay with her and Olive (Olive was Aunt Maude's daughter). They will take good care of me and I promise I will be fine. Please. I can stay on as organist at the church. Besides, I am not a child any more. Please!"

Her pleas were futile. By the first week in September, the life she had known was over. Jana felt she was dumped, along with her little sister and parents, into a large, cold, barren room with nothing more than the beds and a fireplace. At least her brother had a room of his own. Jana's expression of disappointment brought her mother's admonition: "Be grateful Aunt Rose is willing to take us in. That is wonderful of her, you know."

It was not wonderful. Aunt Rose did not like children of any age. Three somewhat rowdy siblings, one of whom imagined herself to be a great musician, certainly did not add any joy to her life, either. She was not shy of saying as much whenever things got a little out of hand.

Mother suffered a lot. Daddy hung on to life but coughed and coughed and coughed. The doctor called it a cardiac cough. Jana slipped into a state of alternating agitation and despondency, her moods swinging back and forth like the first two movements of Beethoven's Pathetique Sonata.

She spent more and more time alone. There was a piano at the high school and the principal said she could practice on it. That became her

most precious activity. No one bothered her there and she became content to lose herself in her fantasies. One happy thing about high school in Fairmont—it seemed easy compared to Highland Falls. Jana had to walk two miles to get there and to be in class by 7:30 in the morning. But she was free by 1:00 in the early afternoon, allowing lots of time for practicing the piano.

After church one Sunday came another stroke of serendipity. The distraught young girl lagged behind to listen to the organist play the most inspiring Bach composition she had heard, his Prelude and Fugue in G Minor. The pedal part of the fugue seemed to be like stairs leading inexorably up, up, and up into the keyboards, right hand first, then left, then pedals again, until it seemed to burst out in the glory of heaven itself. The organist then turned and saw Jana.

"Hello, are you new here?" she asked with what struck Jana as the smile of an angel. "Can I help you?"

Jana was so touched with the offer she was tongue tied at first and could only smile back. This was the beginning of another deep friendship, this time with a lovely lady named Thelma Loudin, a friendship centered typically around this inexplicable wonder called music. Almost immediately Jana started taking piano lessons with Thelma, and Thelma got her a job playing piano for the local ballet school so she could pay for her lessons.

Time seemed to slow down again as life became more normal and orderly for Jana. She went to her job as pianist for the local ballet school two afternoons a week, and practiced piano at the Methodist church near Aunt Rose's place on the other days. Daddy still struggled with his cough but the doctor said he saw improvement. She stayed away from

Aunt Rose's as much as she could to escape the unsettling atmosphere of friction and conflict there.

Once, in her escape mode, she remembered tucking Robert Dvorak's Easter Cantata in a box they were bringing from New York. She ran home from school and raced down the steps to the basement where her family's few extra belongings were piled on a table. Finally, under some books, she found the Cantata. Its well-used pages were battered. She had probably played them more than several hundred times. Off she went to the piano in the church drawing room with this prize manuscript tucked under her arm. Especially the last few pages comforted her. The release from death permeated her very soul when she heard in her mind the softly soaring notes of the coloratura obbligato. Jana recalled the look of pure peace on Lola's face as she gave voice to her husband's composition and the music rose higher and higher until it was almost out of reach. The ecstatic sound made Jana envision the soul being elevated to the heights of heaven with angels in escort.

Once more Jana pondered the mystery. What do I hear in this music? It is peace. It is joy. Where does it really exist and where does it come from? Jana was transfixed by the beauty as she played and remembered. Something was stirring deep in her spirit, in some far corner where only the most intimate thoughts resided, thoughts of life and death and first causes. She thought back to when she was in the grip of a terrible fever, fighting for over a week to stay alive just to hear a moving piece of music twice a day. How did music hold this life-giving and life-saving power in its sounds? To Jana, music's ascendancy, power, and beauty were still things to live for. How did Robert's cantata bring peace to her amidst the confusion and anxiety that surrounded her?

Jana's reverie was broken by a glorious sound that reminded her of Lola's lyrical coloratura at the end of the cantata. She opened the drawing room door. Coming down the hall was Thelma Loudin, singing the Bell Song from Leo Delibes' opera, *Lakme*. What a voice, and what a striking beauty!

Thelma, Jana learned, besides being organist and choir director at the church, was a member of the state board of education. Involved in local politics, she was leading a fight to gain status for married female teachers in the county schools and was working to keep at bay the communist influence that was encroaching in the local college.

It began to dawn on Jana that music perhaps had a kind of supremacy in the order of things—in human health, in philosophy, and who knew what more. In Thelma's case, Jana wondered, could music have an important bearing on her grace and the quiet way that made her so respected and such a major player in the community?

Chapter 10

Cadenza: Different Kinds of Storms

*L*ife settled into a rather rhythmic routine. Jana was trying to take some comfort in the monotony of it, convincing herself that it eased the stresses and turmoil of her family life. Fortunately, however, a bright new chapter opened up for her one afternoon when she went, as usual, to the church to practice.

She entered the church hall and heard a piano being played as she had not heard it since Paul left West Point. Where were the free and fluid sounds, like waves spilling on the seashore, coming from? She opened the door to the drawing room but no one was there. No, farther away, upstairs. She ran up the back stairs to the sanctuary. She stood there transfixed, the familiar chills coursing through her body whenever she experienced the sheer opulence of such beautiful sound.

She stole into a far pew, sat down, and listened. First she heard the breathless romance of a melody mingled with incessant waves of sound. Then the music seemed to raise a question—a vague perception of impend-

ing doom. Indeed the storm struck. Crashing arpeggios did not hide, soaring through them, a version of the initial romantic song, but in anguish this time.

The man at the piano, in front of the choir loft, seemed to Jana to be playing as if his heart would break. He sensed her presence, turned, gave her a smile, and asked if she played the piano, too. He was Walt Rybeck, a reporter for the Fairmont Times, working between semesters at Antioch College.

Jana kept staring at the remarkably large gap between Walt's upper front teeth that made his smile intriguing to her. After an awkward pause, she introduced herself and said, "Yes, I have played for a long time. I love playing piano. I would like to go to music school when I finish high school this year, but my father is very ill."

She chatted on, as if trying to tell her whole life history to this stranger. He listened as if they were old friends and she was captivated by his obvious interest. It turned out they both came often to the church to practice, but at different times. In spite of her youthful innocence, or perhaps because of it, Jana sensed that her excitement at meeting Walt was because of the music. She asked him, "What was that wonderful piece? I would like to learn it."

"It's the Etude in D Flat Major by Liszt, also called *Un Sospiro*—a sigh. It's difficult but I bet you can learn it."

By way of saying goodbye, he played a Schubert Impromptu in A Flat Major. It sped over the keys like a swallow, swooping and diving, and singing the whole way, leaving Jana breathless at the final chords.

For the next several days Jana would rush after school to the church only to be met by silence, and disappointment that no one was there. Not

34

Thelma, not Walt. But after a week she was rewarded by hearing the Impromptu filling the sanctuary with glorious sound. He had brought hot chocolate and doughnuts to share and something else which became one of Jana's prized possessions—a Schirmer's edition of piano duets. It included the beautiful Pearl Fishers by Bizet, a marvelous Mussorgsky piece, and Grieg's Anitra's Dance. For several months it was a frequent occurrence for Jana and Walt to meet and make music together.

Walking together at times, he opened up a new kind of music to her, the songs and chirps of the birds, each species with its recognizably distinct rhythms, tones, and melodies. He introduced Jana to folk music, too, when he let her join a group on a weekend trip to the Jackson's Mill 4-H camp. Under the tutelage of Walt and others, scores of young people joined to dance the Israeli Hora, the Swedish Hambo, polkas, mazurkas, and Appalachian mountain dances.

Jana persuaded Thelma to let her start learning the pieces Walt played. What ecstatic joy to beat into submission those devilish runs in the Lizst until they were doable. Jana set her mind on playing it for her May graduation.

In spring days Jana walked four or five miles into the country where Thelma lived. One day her mother urged her not to go because the radio warned of severe thunder storms. In the teenager's usual headstrong way, she said, "I will not miss my lesson. Besides, the sky isn't even cloudy."

After her lesson, Jana climbed the big hill behind her teacher's house to watch the strange clouds gathering in the southwest. They had an odd color—greenish, grayish, pink, and purple. They were far away, maybe above the next town of Shinnston. It began to sprinkle and the wind whipped up. Angry clouds seemed to be skirting Fairmont and building to the northeast now. A wildness in the air exhilarated Jana.

Suddenly the sky off in the distance turned much darker and lightning began to flash out of the purple clouds. Then an astounding thing happened. A greenish-gray funnel-shaped cloud dropped from one of the thunderheads and started dancing a dervish toward Shinnston. It swayed and undulated like a Persian dancer—extremely lovely to watch and the rhythm of it was captivating.

A streak of lightning hit the ground in explosive power and the earth-shaking rumble rolled across the miles between her and the storm. "Is this what they mean by the music of the spheres?" Jana wondered as she was transfixed by the raw beauty of the sounds emanating from the ferocious storm.

The whipping wind in her face and the rain made brunette noodles of her hair. How she loved it. She felt some connections between the storm's low-throated growl and the thunderous crashing of the left-hand motifs in the Lizst middle section.

Both the storm and the Lizst stirred emotions that Jana felt in her being but could not decipher. Were there connections between nature, life, and music? Could music be a key to otherwise unfathomable relationships? First causes entered her mind again. She did not know, in those days, about Einstein or how he was driven by the conviction that there were first causes and that the secrets of the universe lay in very simple and grandly designed terms. Nor did she have any idea that much of the scientific world had already started down new roads toward discovering the genesis of the universe. Nor was she aware of the coming ideological struggles over whether science or faith, or both, or neither, would yield more insights into first causes. And she certainly had no idea that those same searching questions and the quest to find truth in music would become a driving force in her mature life. To Jana's young mind, no con-

flict appeared between science, faith, and music. And it was becoming part of her thinking that the earth itself was so filled to the brim with majestic music that it must exist by some divine design.

It was May and graduation time. Jana reflected on her school years. Her entire childhood was marked by intelligent advantage and abilities to comprehend beyond her age level. She had spent half a year in the first grade and only a few weeks in the third grade before she was promoted into fourth grade because she was so bored with the third grade curriculum. And now it was graduation time and she was just past her sixteenth birthday.

A few weeks earlier, Jana had played the Lizst concert etude and some Bach inventions in a competition for a full scholarship to West Virginia University in Morgantown. She was awarded alternate first place. Her nemesis was a student of the piano department's chairperson. A newspaper column alluding to the unfairness of this was sweet release for Jana, but it made no impact on the powers that be. No matter. Her parents were returning to Highland Falls and Jana felt certain they would insist that she return, too. They could not deal with the idea of letting her be on her own. So Jana played the Lizst for graduation, but it was an anticlimax. She was feeling tossed around, weary and empty, leaving everything behind one more time.

Her mother and two siblings went to New York first. Mother wrote triumphantly that she had found a house for all of them, that she had her old job back at the tailor shop, that Jana and daddy should come by train as soon as possible, and that all was well. But not for Jana. When she met Walt at the Methodist church one last time, she confessed she didn't want to go to New York and felt like running away. Feeling her anguish,

he assured her this would be an interlude, not the end. He said he looked forward to hearing about her next adventures with music.

Although Jana's father had improved enough to go back home, it was obvious he would never work again. Jana's blue mood made her imagine spending the rest of her life supporting her ailing and aging parents. They were not that old, but she could not see beyond the possibility that, as the oldest child, care-taking responsibilities would fall on her shoulders.

Chapter 11

DA CAPO: ANOTHER ABRUPT ENDING

The evening was hot, muggy, dark, and raining hard. Uncle Bob, daddy's kid brother, had been a close friend through all of this, too, and he brought daddy to the train station. Leaving Fairmont, Jana had avoided having to say goodbye to Aunt Rose by meeting Walt downtown. They walked under his umbrella down Virginia Avenue and across the bridge toward the station. Part way down the steep hill, Walt suddenly pulled Jana into the shelter of a doorway, lowered his umbrella and gave her a warm hug.

"I shall miss you, you know." Just as quickly, the umbrella was furled and they ran speedily down the rest of the hill, getting quite wet and laughing like little children.

The Pullman car stopped exactly where the little party—Uncle Bob, daddy, Walt and Jana—stood waiting on the platform. The conductor took the bags and helped daddy on the train.

"All abooaard!" and the first lurch of the steam engine pulling its load struck the finality of the scene into Jana's mind. The end of a lovely piece of

music, she thought. Then she remembered that cream and yellow bedroom, years back, where a little girl found for some yet unknown reason the healing power of music. Everything was returning to the beginning place and it filled the girl with sadness.

Chapter 12

CODA: RESPONSE TO FUTILITY

ike a slow motion movie, daddy gradually improved over the next two years, but clearly not enough to work again. Mother's job at the tailor shop enabled her to carry the burden of keeping the family housed and fed, and of providing for the two younger siblings. Jana went back to teaching piano and playing the organ in the little Highland Falls Methodist Church.

Jana's potential scholarship to Pottsdam was revoked because, having completed high school in West Virginia, she did not have the necessary New York Regents diploma. Curtis Institute was not possible, either, for several reasons, not the least of which was simply that her parents would not even talk about letting her proceed with her schooling away from Highland Falls. To deal with the sense of loss that set in after these major disappointments, her only respite was to practice and practice and practice.

One happy event lifted her spirits. Her dear friend and mentor Robert Dvorak came back to West Point to direct the Army Band when its long-

time director retired. By this time Jana had over thirty piano and organ students, and planning student recitals kept her busy. At some of these recitals, Lola Dvorak would perform as visiting artist, and at others, Jana invited Myron Mayor from the Army Band who played the flute like an angel.

Little by little, nevertheless, a sense of futility won the battle over Jana's natural exuberance. This played no small part in her announcement that she was going to be married. At age eighteen. Silence. She was to find out that in significant ways the last chord had sounded.

Chapter 13

CHACONNE: LITTLE CONSOLATION

"In music, a *chaconne* (Italian: ...*ciaconne*) [is a] fiery and suggestive dance that first appeared in Spain about 1600 AD and eventually gave its name to a musical form. Miguel de Cervantes, Francisco Gomez de Quevedo, and other contemporary writers imply a Mexican origin but do not indicate whether it was indigenous or a Spanish dance modified there. Apparently danced with castanets by a couple or by a woman alone, it soon spread to Italy, where it was considered disreputable as it had been in Spain. During the 16th century, the dance became subdued and stylized, and in the 17th century it gained favor in the French court. The musical form of the *chaconne* is a continuous variation on some repeated short progression."—Encyclopedia Britannica

In retrospect, a particular phase of Jana's life reveals a close affinity to the structure of the chaconne. This was not evident during the years already described, when her life had the rhapsodic qualities of constant change and never-ending innovation. From the time of her first marriage until the late 1960s, however, her life took on the inherent qualities of the chaconne: there

was a repetitive structure to what happened to her during the next two decades along her life's journey when she found herself largely divorced from the one thing that was her cohesive strength—her music—and through that music, some mystical and irrevocable connection with and dedication to the God from Whom that music seemed to emanate.

Just as the chaconne, like a chameleon, changed color over time, she, too, underwent a kind of metamorphosis. Broad-stroked changes, often without her being aware, were shaping her personality and molding her approach to life.

Chapter 14

THEME II: A CHANGE OF KEY
CANTUS FIRMUS I: REPEATED MOTIFS

By definition, a cantus firmus is a pre-existing melody forming the basis of a polyphonic composition.

As a young girl and teenager, Jana was known for her quick wit, dreamy romanticism, sharp tongue, volatile moods and intelligence. Never still, she was in almost perpetual motion, running on her way to West Point, chasing after butterflies, always on the go, except when she was practicing the piano or organ.

In piano music, the ground bass is that pattern in the left hand which gives a piece order, allowing the melody to take flight. The ground bass of Jana's life was music. In some form or other she was always in touch with the harmonies and rhythms of the world around her. This came naturally to her, as intuitive as the robin sweetening its song at eventide. She sensed a continuing and constant force that drove her. She suspected she was attuned in some way to the energy of the world. What that energy was comprised of, she had no idea. The sensations and the questions they raised were themes that kept re-

peating themselves and animated many of her waking moments. Even in sleep, her mind wandered to vast territories where beauty and energy were one and the same and where the music around her, more than aesthetically pleasing, struck her as the lifeblood of the entire universe.

Jana's family worried at times about her mental stability. Her friends endured her tirades and fantasies, excusing them as the fruits of a creative and energetic soul. Her pastors accused her of more than a normal share of sexual drive. Her first husband and the father of her children had more than his share of attempts—attempts that did not work—to tame her.

Her marriage marked a time of divorcement from Jana's intense love affair with music, though not entirely. She played piano or organ in various and sundry churches. She gave lessons when money was scarce, which was most of the time. At one point she taught at an unaccredited Bible college for $250 a month. Yet there was no study, no Paul Shocker, no Robert Dvorak, no Walt Rybeck, no recitals, and no concerts.

Rather, for many years she was thrust into—one might almost say *imprisoned in*—a fundamentalist society that looked down on classical music. This music that Jana held most dear was considered a worldly thing to be feared and avoided, along with playing cards, dancing, or innocent friendships with one's best friend's husband. When Jana's beloved Lester piano fell off a pick-up truck and shattered in a mishap of titanic proportions, she could not help wondering whether it was really an accident. The music she was permitted to play was associated with a kind of piety and religiosity that annoyed her intensely. Her husband had always held a strong distaste for her devotion to classical music, and this horrible loss occurred while the piano was being moved by Don, his cousins, and the pastor.

Jana's first pregnancy ended with a miscarriage that devastated her. Then, just after her twentieth birthday, her daughter Gail arrived. The baby's crying made the father so angry that Jana turned to her mother for solace: "I'm miserable," she confessed. "Being a mother scares me to death. I don't know how to make Gail stop crying, or how to cope with her father's anger. I don't even play the piano anymore. What am I going to do?"

She later learned that her mother, like Jana herself, had been deeply hurt by the vicissitudes of life, for which she had found no good answers. But now, in response, all her mother could offer were trite maxims: "Do the best you can. Women are meant to be mothers. You will learn. Besides," she added, "I told you not to marry him, didn't I?"

Nancy, Jana's second daughter, arrived sixteen months later. Son Kenneth came along five years after that. The ground bass kept haunting Jana. The old themes kept recurring. The throbbing rhythms of the universe still beat in her temples. By the time Kenneth was two and Gail and Nancy were in school, Jana's husband was pastoring a small church in western New York. A lady there was a ray of sunshine. Mary Shurtleff somehow understood what they had not discussed, that Jana was mourning the separation from her music, so she offered a quiet suggestion.

"Maybe you could squirrel away some of your grocery money for a while, enough to pay for piano lessons at Houghton College where there is a marvelous teacher. And I'll tell you what—I'll keep the children while you're taking lessons and no one will ever need to know."

Jana did just that. All went well until she had to admit to her husband that her mandatory recital was only a couple of months away. He was more than a little displeased. Only after a lot of shouting and pleading was it finally agreed she could play her recital. The complaining, how-

ever, continued. "These music studies are a ridiculous waste. We are so short of money. Why are you spending our grocery money on piano lessons? Believe me, I'm going to have to find a way to put a stop to this."

"You can't stop me," Jana fought back. "If you try, I will take the children and go back to my parents. I never should have married you."

She also appealed to her husband, since he was a pastor, with a theological argument. Quoting Eldon Basney, her teacher, she said, "Basney says that I have real talent, that God gave me this talent, and that I must not think of giving up my music."

The quarrels were often out of control. Shouting turned into tirades. Bad things happened which frightened the children, and Jana, too. These first gusts gathered into a storm which in a few years destroyed the marriage. What kept Jana from utter despair in these dark times was the relentless playing over and over in her mind the role of music in her life, the music that Basney said she must not give up. The music that Robert, Paul, and Walt had joined in loving with her—for her—and had caused her to understand it as a necessity in life.

During this period the first seeds of an idea were sown in her heart and intellect—a quest to unravel where music had come from and to fathom its mysterious power. This was more than an intellectual excursion. At the start it was a quasi-spiritual experience. No doubt she entered this out-of-mind realm because certain stimuli—melodies, rhythms, crescendos, diminuendos, harmonies, and progressions—triggered that familiar chill up and down her body. Something significant and deep within her soul was being touched. How often she remembered with a sense of longing the yellow and blue bedroom where wrenchingly beautiful music had kept her alive until her body could heal itself. No matter how hard she tried to bring back that special music, it evaded her.

She bought a new copy of Beethoven's sonatas and began to refresh the *Pathetique* which she had learned years before. Its wild gyrations of mood and emotion felt like a personal expression of her life. During those days when the family was living in church parlors, she often played the children to sleep by practicing this wonderful work. Her husband would be out in the church office while she was alone with her children and the piano. These were good moments.

In much the same way that the chaconne evolved from an indelicate dance-song into a subdued and stylized court dance, Jana experienced a change in her style of facing life. Frenetic and sometimes hostile responses to frustration and dissatisfaction softened. She began to evolve into a mature woman who could trust her own intelligence instead of being afraid of it. The bleakness of her daily existence remained, but the maturity paradoxically enabled her to recapture some of the innocent vibrancy of her youth. In this more confident mood, music once more became new every day and the world seemed literally held together by the beauty of it.

There were other powerful musical metaphors in Jana's repertoire of piano works that held special meaning for her. For instance, the end of Bach's Chaconne in D Minor—after thirty-one sets of variations which express the haunting allure and deep longing of its original theme in ever-intensifying and ever-elevating passion—returns to the inexplicable power of that original theme. It does so in a way that presents itself as a resolution bathed in reality. Nothing in the theme itself has changed. It is still the same progression, the same rhythmic identity, the same expression of the human dilemma, sad and pervasive. But the majestic breadth of the chords, now expanded to the bursting point—largamente, maestoso, pesante, sempre piu allargando—and rooted in grandeur give

hope to the spirit. Even in its melancholy, it is confident, especially in the one edition in which the very last chord is suddenly and magnificently dropped into the major mode. Longing abruptly anchored in the strength of that final D major chord. It is finished.

"There is something ahead," Jana thought, "something that the variations in my life are leading toward but that I can't put my finger on. I must wait and see."

Chapter 15

DECEPTIVE CADENCE: A FALSE ENDING?

The end of Jana's particular chaconne came in 1968, at least temporarily, when she divorced her husband, the father of her children.

Waiting in the wings was a man who had cared for Jana and the children through the divorce and the bad times preceding it. Lt. Col. Earle W. Hutchison was an army chaplain at Fort Jackson, South Carolina, where the family had lived for eight years after moving from New York. Jana met him when she became organist at his chapel. He was also divorced. Seventeen years older than Jana, he had a huge heart but curiously an inability to relate intimately to others. He was reclusive but kind and loved well from a distance. He was intellectual, scholarly, and a bit on the effete side.

For a couple of years, while Jana's husband was succumbing to a breakdown, Hutchison had been standing in the breach. He would leave groceries in Jana's car or on the doorstep of their modest house, and Jana later learned that he had secretly paid the mortgage and car payments.

Also, Hutchison clearly was very taken with his organist who was vibrant and, comparatively, young. He picked her up one terribly rainy day during the divorce proceedings and drove her to a grove of pine trees near the post chapel. The rain was coming down in sheets as he parked his huge old DeSoto, reached into the glove compartment, took out a black velvet box, and handed it to Jana.

"This is for you because you are such a good mother to your children and because you are so good to be around." Jana would never forget these words or the wonder of the gift to which they were a prelude. In the box was a bracelet of three rows of aurora borealis crystals set in sterling silver.

She looked at him in amazement as her mind raced back to her intense sensations from a real aurora, sensations so special she had not tried to describe them to anyone, not even Hutchison. What were the odds of his choosing such a gift? Jana was so filled with emotion that her tongue would only let her utter, rather lamely, "Thank you, they are so beautiful." In fact, neither then nor to the day the colonel died, did Jana ever find the words to explain her mystical encounter with the northern lights that made her so touched by the aurora crystals Hutchison gave her.

The divorce decree was finalized in December 1968. Hutchison met Jana outside her attorney's office and took her to the Columbia airport for dinner. He knew that because of her passion for flying airplanes, the airport was a favorite place for her to go when there was serious thinking to be done. Once in front of the main terminal, he took Jana's hand, looked into her eyes and with great ceremony asked her to honor him to be his wife.

Chapter 16

MODULATION: RETURN TO THEME I
THE NEW WORLD SYMPHONY: IN MINIATURE

Jana had never quite figured out this man who was usually inscrutable and remote, but at times quite accessible. He could be funny and sarcastic, kind but upsetting. Jana knew he loved her, but how to categorize that love? Not filial, because it was physical. Not intimate, because it was caring but not romantic. He truly cared for her and her children, but in a rather fatherly way. Was his effeteness a mitigating factor or was it simply that the colonel could only love from afar because of his own hurts?

A week after his proposal they were married—the beginning of vast changes in Jana's life. Suddenly all decisions were made unilaterally by Earle. If he met her at the door with a ready-made whiskey sour for her, Jana came to know for sure something large was afoot, something that may or may not have been to her liking. At least she learned to enjoy the whiskey sours.

The changes were more encompassing than Jana could know at the time they were taking place. Certainly, many were changes for the better. The

abject poverty and daily confusion of the first marriage were gone. She had no longer to fear uncertainty, hunger, anger, or emotional unsteadiness because of the volatile personality of her children's father. She was freed from the stifling authoritarianism of the Puritanical mind-set that she had grown so accustomed to. Hutchison did not seem to mind that his wife preferred bikinis to one-piece bathing suits.

But the most life-changing differences had more to do with her position in the scheme of things. She was no longer in control of anything. Decisions were made for her, even down to "you will have your own checking account and I will show you how to maintain it."

While enjoying the freedom from super-religiosity which had little to do with real faith, she still felt constricted and held down. It was perplexing to feel free and imprisoned at the same time. She could be herself, for once, as long as being herself did not violate the obvious responsibility to continue becoming more and more mature. Education was a large issue. There were obviously correct ways of doing things that had to be observed. She did her best and tried to enjoy the benefits of getting a good education and having enough money.

Gail went to Charleston, South Carolina to live with her father while Jana, Earle, and the two younger children remained in Columbia. Earle retired from the Army and was looking for a teaching position in the local schools. One winter evening Jana came home to find Earle waiting with the famous whiskey sour. When he asked her to sit on the sofa and make herself comfortable, that only made her uncomfortable and apprehensive.

"Is anything wrong?" she asked.

Earle replied, "Heavens no. I just thought you might be interested in this." He handed her the latest Chaplain's News with an ad in block print, circled in red:

Chapter 16

HOW WOULD YOU LIKE TO RETIRE TO A SMALL CHURCH ON THE JERSEY SHORE?

Jana was stunned. She had grown fond of South Carolina. She had never learned to care for the Northeast corridor. Something in her southern heritage was not at home in the Yankee atmosphere. Even as a child at West Point—much as she relished her teachers and the musical experiences—she had felt vaguely out of place there.

Yet within two weeks, the die was cast. Jana and Earle went to Lavallette, New Jersey for a kind of audition at which the Reverend Colonel Hutchison preached to the congregation. He was so good at what he did that his acceptance was a fait accompli. Within a few months, he, Jana, and son Kenneth were living in the manse in Lavallette.

Meanwhile Gail began living with a young Navy man in Charleston. Nancy, sixteen and a high school senior with a job at the telephone company, adamantly declared she was not going to New Jersey. Unlike Jana's parents, she and Earle agreed with their child and found a strict Methodist boarding home for her in Columbia where she could be safe and well cared for.

Freed at last from domestic turmoil and tormenting financial pressures, Jana began to notice a change in her thoughts. She found that the beach, after all, was a wonderful place to meditate and ponder memories that flooded back to her:

…That blue and yellow bedroom…the power of music that kept her alive for weeks…and what was that composition she still had not found again anywhere?

…The delight of the Army band selections…even if Paul Schocker called their arrangements of symphonies, tone poems, and concertos "abortions" because, for instance, they dared to try to make clarinets into violins.

…The deep swish-splash, swish-splash of the ocean waves reminded Jana of the power of the huge Moeller organ in the West Point Chapel…20 years later she still recalled how that immense granite building vibrated when Marcel Dupre, the great French organist, played the 32-foot pedal stop.

…The magic 1940s when Robert, Paul, Walt, Thelma, Frederick, and others opened to her the world of Bach, Brahms, Mussorgsky, Chopin, and so many more wonderful composers.

…The many voices of nature, as if struggling for equilibrium… the varied bird calls, the deep rumble of thunder after lightning flashes…and the dances of nature—the clouds, the wind-blown trees, the aurora borealis.

…The rich velvety sound of the Westminster Choir as she sat with her father in the balcony of the West Point gymnasium…she did not know then that the director, John Finley Williamson, was a lion among choral conductors, but he and the choir astounded her, inspiring her to think, "I want to do that when I am older, sing or conduct, to somehow be part of that kind of beauty."

…Thirty of her forty years in one way or another had been steeped in the beauty, power, and ethereal quality of music. She had come to feel that music was an ineffable ingredient of life, eternally evident on the earth and perhaps the entire universe. She recalled reading in the Psalms that the "morning stars sang together" and wondering what that meant.

...Remarkable, Jana thought, are the rhythms of her own body—waking, sleeping, breathing, pulsating. And the cosmic rhythms, too—the seasons, night and day, the revolutions and orbits of the earth, sun, moon and other planets, stars and galaxies.

As a pastor's wife, she had few friends and an abundance of time to think about such things. Two of Jana's children were going about their lives without her. Her son and husband both tended to be remote from her. The one cohesive force in her life was music. In the fall of 1970 Jana joined a community chorus led by Charles Read, a graduate of Westminster Choir College in Princeton. Things began to change quickly.

Jana tired of the sameness of the repertory and the political squabbles of the community chorus so she mentioned to Earle that she would like to go to school. She had spent years, during her troubled first marriage, in psychological counseling and loved the sense of healing that came from talking. She felt she would like to help others as she had been at least partially healed by several counselors. She matriculated at the local community college, spending a year and half studying psychology.

That year and a half opened Jana's mind to possibilities of all kinds. She was glad to be expelled from the cocoon of religious authoritarianism into an atmosphere of learning and challenge. She was glad to have her mind titillated with things scholarly that she knew nothing about. And that was the beginning of the growth of mind and spirit that would eventually lead Jana to where she found herself at the age of 75—immersed in a project so overwhelming in its scope that she sometimes buckled under the weight of it.

Earle was not convinced that the study of psychology was right for her. A counselor himself, he had keen insights and a smooth way of guiding: "Jana, you are a talented musician already, and perhaps spend-

ing your time on this new pursuit is ill-advised. You are not really young anymore."

That stung Jana.

He continued, "I wonder if music school would not be a better fit for you."

It sounded like a question, but from Earle it was really a statement of fact. He had made up his mind, his thought rang true, and there was nothing left but to accept it. So he packed Jana into the car and took her to Princeton for entrance exams into Westminster Choir College. Then she took the long College Level Evaluation Program tests. She "CLEP'd" out of an entire year, enabling Jana to enter Westminster as a sophomore.

She was excited as she stepped into the role of music student in September 1972. Her vagrant wonderings and full memory bank gave her much to probe and talk about with her new teachers and colleagues. Of course, her fellow students were clearly not her peers since she was old enough to be their mother.

Her first meeting with Dr. Joseph Flummerfelt, director of choral activities, was memorable. He was tall, not necessarily handsome, but with craggy good looks and a commanding presence. One would not want to get on his bad side. Though his manner was stern, Jana noticed that his eyes twinkled.

Earlier, Jana, after long and arduous conversations, had convinced the director of the Chapel Choir that she had had enough choral experience to sidestep the mandatory one year in the "farm" choir which required the allegiance of every new Westminster novitiate. Possibly she prevailed because of her age. At any rate, she found herself standing in front of Dr. Flummerfelt for an audition to join the renowned Westminster Choir. Untypically, she was surprised at feeling very nervous. It made her wonder if she should not have talked her way out of the chapel choir. "My sight reading is awful, my rhythm is terrible, and my voice will crack. What am I doing here?" None of this was true, but "Flum," as the choir called him, interrupted her self doubts.

He looked at her with his piercing eyes that twinkled in spite of himself, handed her a book of Bach chorales, gave her a page number, gave her a pitch, and asked her to sing the tenor part. Jana could not recall which chorale it was or how it was that she actually stayed on her feet. When she finished, he took the book and said nothing. Her heart sank. Then he gave her another assignment:

"Here is a pitch. Sing this scale up one octave and back down without taking breath. Any tempo, on 'la.'" That exercise went off without trouble. Flum gave her another pitch and told her to sing that scale on "ah" up and down. When she finished Flum smiled and said, "I should have heard a break at about 'sol' but I did not. Do you always have such success with your register changes?"

Jana left the office in a state of suspended animation. She couldn't really tell what had happened or whether it was good or bad. Several days later the list of names forming the new Westminster Choir for the year was posted. Jana's name was there! And in her mailbox was a note from Dr. Flummerfelt asking her to see him in his office. She climbed the three flights of stairs as if on wings.

Before she was in his open door he welcomed Jana into the choir, saying, "I hope it will be one of the cardinal experiences of your life," and he proceeded to critique her audition. "You have a lovely voice, untrained, but that will change. The quality is good and even. No big breaks evident. I have taken you into the choir mainly because of the

timbre of your voice. You say you have always sung tenor. The voices of our young singers in many cases have not settled yet. What I need in my mezzo section is more depth or richness or—that is, your voice has the advantage of age—what I mean, it is more, uh…"

"You mean," Jana laughed, "because I am older, I have richer timbre?"

Dr. Flummerfelt knew he may have misspoken, but he laughed, too, and the moment passed. Now they were friends. It was soon obvious that Flum loved his students and, even more, he loved the beauty they were able to create together. Jana was intrigued by the deep and binding relationships that grew out of this association and wondered if they reflected—besides the joy of performing wonderful music—something even more potent.

Chapter 17

An Old World Opera: In Italian

Becoming a student opened another life-changing event for Jana. The Westminster Choir was the choir in residence at the Festival of Two Worlds in Spoleto, Italy. She was not prepared for the magnitude of the impact that being part of this festival would have on her. Her first visit there in the spring of 1973 was like living in a dream.

Rehearsals started the day after the choir landed in Italy, with no time to get acclimated to the new environment. They worked on Giacomo Puccini's opera, *Manon Lescaut*, which was to be the highlight of the entire festival. The students were faced with very serious professional stagecraft, a contrast to their usual choir rehearsal atmosphere. A somewhat intimidating surprise was hearing that the great Luchino Visconti would direct the opera. Advanced in years, he was still a formidable personage. He sat in a balcony at the back of the small theater, watching Maestro Thomas Schippers put the choir through its paces. Jana could not take her eyes off Visconti as he sat there, bundled in a mohair wrap.

The choir women were divided into two groups of actors. One set was cast as elegant and cultured ladies, the others as "girls" whose dress and demeanor would make it clear what kind of loose girls they were. In the opening scene, Des Grieux, the chevalier, is flirting with the girls and Visconti chose one of them to be the lucky fanciula, or young girl, who would be the main target of Des Grieux's flirtations.

Later, when they were rehearsing in costume, Visconti called out loudly, waving his hands at Maestro Schippers: "Stopp-a the music-a! This-a will never do!" Pointing to the fanciula, he said, "This-a lady, she is-a too elegant." Indeed she was tall and aristocratic looking, not the working girl type called for in the role of "girl of the streets."

"I need a more—ah, degraded-a looking one," Visconti said. "That-a one will do. Si, she is-a good," and he pointed directly at Jana! The entire cast had a good laugh over that.

Performing *Manon Lescaut* four or five times a week for a month, Jana found it humbling and incredibly moving to sing under Thomas Schippers' direction, to watch Visconti at work, and to be associated with some of the finest opera stars of Italy and the United States. Critics said that this 1973 Spoleto season was a pinnacle year for the festival.

During her stay, Jana and Bea, another student, shared a room in the private home of a woman named Anna. They reached it from the central piazza through a narrow cobbled street, under archways, past houses with window boxes overflowing with blossoms, and down a hill to a larger archway that fronted on a large dark entranceway. Urns filled with plants and the smell of damp stones and moss greeted them. It was like walking into the pages of a medieval novel as they passed through a wrought iron gate into the house. Inside was all dark wood above glistening white

marble floors. The furnishings were large and stately. Their bedroom was sparsely furnished, but elegant with crisp white linens on the bed.

On their arrival, a little girl of eleven, named Anna like her mother, bounced into the room chattering away. "Buono pomeriggio. Come va? Piacere. Come si chiama? E' la prima volta che visit gli Italia?" She had no idea that Bea and Jana did not understand Italian. Jana said the only words she knew, "Io buono," in a way that made Anna laugh. That broke the ice and Anna was a constant visitor over the next couple months.

The town of Spoleto lies in the Umbrian hills. To Jana the town was a nugget of culture and loveliness contrasting with the ugliness of so much of the world. She was amazed at the old ladies who sang every morning as they prepared their fruit and vegetable stands. How did they know the arias from the Italian masters? And how, she wondered, can they sing so effortlessly what the choir must struggle to learn? When the police would storm through the streets with their sirens screaming DA-DA-DA-DA, peace would return quickly and one would hear singing everywhere.

The students took advantage of time off to travel around. Jana felt she was bathing in antiquity as she visited the duomo—the "cathedral"—in every village, the Hermitage in Assisi, Michelangelo's seemingly alive statue of David in Florence, and the Vatican and so many sights in Rome.

Above all else, Jana was thrilled with the music. Wonderful concerts. A special event each summer was a party at the home of Gian Carlo Menotti, the founder of the Spoleto festival and a great American composer.

The choir had been alerted that the maestro was somewhat reserved and should not be approached too aggressively or too openly. Jana was pleasantly surprised to find that she need not have worried over meet-

ing Menotti, because he was the epitome of gentility and warmth. Soft-spoken and manifesting a gentle smile, he met the choir members at the front gate and greeted each one individually with a directness that made everyone feel at ease. Often, during the course of the party, his unaffect-ed laughter could be heard echoing down the marble halls of his elegant villa. He conversed with the choir members with ease and seemed to have an incredible sense of humor. No wonder his music is so accessible, Jana mused.

Every day at vespers the Westminster Choir gathered in the cloister of the duomo and sang Bach chorales. Colonnades and arches supported the roof of the cloister which was open on one side to the sprawling piazza in front of the cathedral. In this place of worship, an idyllic setting, the gran-ite walls caught and magnified the choir's voices, carrying them out to the tourists and locals gathered in the piazza every evening to hear vespers.

Once more, the interaction of the composer, the performers, and the listeners—what she could only describe as a spiritual experience—trig-gered Jana's old quest to probe how music seemed to penetrate one's very soul.

One extraordinary day the choir and Flum were in the duomo again for rehearsal. The sun seemed brighter than usual. Spoleto appeared in-fused with light. Flum seemed in rare high spirits. The choir was re-hearsing Psalm 90 by Charles Ives. An American composer, Ives had a unique ability to portray biblical texts and to depict the cosmos in choral sound. Psalm 90 moves from the hot anger of a wrathful God toward his disobedient servants to the awesome "forgiving-ness" of God and thence to the repentance of the people as they turn back to Him and receive that forgiveness. This psalm also deals with the transitory nature of human life

and the necessity for avoiding God's anger before man's strength is cut off. Ives somehow captures all of this powerful emotion in choral sound.

"Who knoweth the power of thy wrath?" At this point, on the word "wrath," it is uncanny how realistically the vocal sound expresses that wrath. The choir divides into at least eight voices and the cutting dissonance of a huge chord reaching more than two octaves seems to encompass the vastness of God's wrath against sin. On that day, that word "wrath" and that sound from the voices elicited a response from the very building itself. A shaking, transient rumbling grew until it surrounded the astounded singers—and then it was gone. The whole choir experienced a moment of unmitigated fright as the sensation of an earthquake coursed through its ranks. Dr. Flummerfelt responded by deftly ending the great dissonance with a wave of his hand. The choir was stilled and the floor became quiet once more. After this awesome moment, the rehearsal was over. As he dismissed the choir for the day, Flum muttered something, barely audible, about "having heard the voice of God today."

What really happened? For Jana, it brought back that same chill she had had in the blue and yellow room when she felt certain she was kept alive by that exquisite music—music she still had not identified. On the way back to her room in Anna's house, her mind was racing. She recalled Paul Schocker long ago saying that, when tuning his harp, he had to take into account harmonics and overtones. She recalled the myths about great sopranos breaking crystal glasses with their powerful harmonics and overtones. Were these akin to the sympathetic vibrations her eighth grade science teacher described to illustrate the strange collapse of a bridge in Tacoma, Washington? The bridge, called Galloping Gertie, began undulating during a windstorm until the swinging became more violent and the giant span buckled and a large section plunged into

the Puget Sound below. Was there a connection between the rhythm of that bridge and the rhythm of the duomo when touched by the rhythmic vibrations of the music the choir was singing? She believed, yes, this had been an aerodynamic phenomenon of massive proportions, but the chill she had experienced again led her to look for an even deeper meaning.

To Jana, her life mirrored the recurring structure of the chaconne, with uncertainties and mysteries that would only be satisfied when understanding finally dawned. She thought of the powerful Picardy third imposed by Ferruccio Busoni at the end of the towering Bach Chaconne in D Minor. The nature of the "Picardy third"—that is, the sudden shifting from the melancholy and sadness of the minor mode to the strength and assuredness of the major tonality—was magnificently portrayed here by Busoni. All the struggles and warfare of this magnificent work come to an abrupt but satisfying end with that powerful chord in D Major.

Like the augmentations and diminutions in the thematic material of a Bach composition, Jana's life would from now on be punctuated by short periods of clarity followed by prolonged periods of a kind of stagnation while she struggled to express a strong and probably highly controversial theory that gradually had been forming itself in her subconscious. After hearing the sounds of God's voice under her feet in the duomo, Jana did not realize as she walked alone back to her quarters that her life had just changed rather dramatically—during the summer of 1973 in Spoleto, Italy.

66

Chapter 18

CANTUS FIRMUS II

*J*ana's insights into the mystery of music's power began to mesh with her feelings about creation itself. Since much has been described about her musical experiences, understanding her story from this point requires a look at her religious background. Was this preexisting melody the Creation melody written by God Himself—the very melody around which every other embellishment or counterpoint is woven?

It seems that Jana's tenth year was pivotal. She was the eldest of three children born to a fundamentalist family of Southern lineage. Almost by definition, that made them a family of strictest religious standards. The picture is easy to paint: no smoking or drinking, no make-up for the women, no dancing or card playing, no mention whatever of the word "sex," no flashy dresses or garb of any kind, and, certainly, no open attachments to the world, the flesh, and the devil! Sundays were spent in "worship" and restful activities at home or at church. And never, but never, read the Sunday funnies until after school on Monday afternoon. All of this negative thinking didn't make

sense to a vivacious little girl whose curiosity drove her night and day. Her imagination was so vivid that three imaginary playmates were her natural companions far into her late childhood. In fact, she and they had more fun than she and most of her real friends.

In spite of the legalistic approach to raising their children which was taken by her parents, Jana was aware that they loved her and her two siblings, and, certainly, both her mother and her father were always very present in the home. But there was a gap, a kind of vacuum, in the emotional fabric of the family, especially where her mother was concerned. That may have explained, partially at least, the three imaginary friends— who, by the way, were airplane pilots—and the prolific creative energy which Jana seemed to expend so easily in weaving the tales of adventure she experienced with Pit, Ginory, and Mud.[i]

The thin emotional fabric of the family was offset by constant exposure to the Bible, its stories and its proclamations of deliverance from heartache and disquiet, and the granting of that peace that "passes all understanding" to those who needed it and sought it. It would be a long time before Jana could see that what the Bible said was infinitely true

---

[i]   *It was not until very much later in her life that Jana would realize how she first invented these three amazing people. Their names had an incredible genesis. Jana's daddy loved airplanes and often took her, her baby brother, and her mother down to Amarillo on Sunday afternoons to watch the barnstormers fly at the Amarillo Airport. On a particular Sunday, as they watched, a big, strange looking airplane flew in. It had a huge round engine on the front like any other aircraft. It had wings with tips that pointed up to the sky. That was odd, but the strangest thing about it was that high over its open cockpit were four huge blades like a helicopter's blades that went 'round and 'round. A tiny, blonde woman climbed down from the cockpit of the mud-covered machine and walked up to Jana and her family.*

"Hello, little girl! Do you like my airplane? That's a Pitcairn autogiro! Someday you will learn to fly one of those."

It was Amelia Earhart! A Pitcairn autogiro, all covered with mud—Pit, Ginory, and Mud.

Although adventures of this ilk had little, if anything, to do with Jana's musical bent, they certainly did have a great deal to do with the expansion of her intellect and imagination.

and really did counter the mundane-ness and anxiety of her everyday life and would ultimately give her hope for this world and eternity. But this is where "it" started—her quest for beauty and truth. In her young mind there was only an untrodden path to reconciling her unrest with the rest and peace of the Bible. She had to find "it," that she knew. And the only vehicle that came close to giving her respite was her music.

The little church that she and her family attended had an early twentieth century charm that enchanted her. The homely, bull-dog-faced preacher stood several steps above the floor of the pew area where a podium all carved of dark oak wood successfully separated him from the commoners below. This whole panorama was sheltered under an arch which spanned more than twenty feet, and the ceiling of it was probably twenty feet high. Fifteen or twenty feet behind him and far above his head was the most beautiful stained-glass window in the shape of a rose and a-glint with jewel colors which caught the sun and splashed those colors all over the floor of the area where he stood. Painted in deep pastels on the front of that arch, from one end to the other, were the words "Worship Him In The Beauty Of Holiness". There were flowers intertwined with the words. Jana teased herself during the unending sermons by wondering if it were the preacher that was supposed to be worshipped. She decided not. But, then, this great God, Who was to be "praised in the beauty of holiness", where was He and how would one find Him? And what did He have to do with us, anyway? It was all a great mystery. Except that Jana had been taught that Jesus had been sent by Him to give us a way to understand that He did love us and would look after us. And then, what was this "beauty of holiness"?

One other artifact in the altar area emblazoned itself on Jana's memory. It was the dark oak communion table where the bread and wine of the

communion sacrament were placed the first Sunday of every month. The face of the table was beautifully carved with the words "In Remembrance Of Me." Jana knew that the communion was some kind of symbol of the death and resurrection of Jesus Christ, but she was not quite able to grasp what the true meaning of all this was. But, thanks to the beautiful table and its message, she knew she had to "remember" it.

It was during this tenth year that Jana began to feel the pull of something deep within her soul somewhere, even though she was not sure what a soul was, and she began to try to find a path to follow to the truth that she intuited must exist. Heavy stuff for a little girl but then she had always been very precocious, hadn't she?

The Bible stories and scripture verses which were so undeniably the warp and woof of Jana's childhood development never left her. As a matter of fact, as she matured, they became more and more necessary to her way of life. They were her standard and became the very principles by which she acted and reacted. And all of this without her conscious avowal. She just knew that whatever the Bible said had to have validity, and somehow, somewhere, she would be able to see that validity for herself instead of just having to believe it because the preacher, or her mom or dad, said so. There was a power so strong in the statements made so succinctly in the Bible that Jana could never bring herself to disavow them, at any rate. So they took root in her soul and served as a rudder to guide her when she had not an idea which way to turn.

It probably was the presence of unrecognized, unresolved, and misguided understanding of truth that led her into marrying not one, but two, preachers. Preachers should have the answers, after all, shouldn't they? Unfortunately, it took Jana nearly a lifetime to discover that truth lay in Creation itself, and that the keys to understanding were all in the

warp and woof of the universe, put there irrefutably by the great God Creator Himself.

If He were the great Creator God, then all of creation would have to have His finger prints upon it, the rules of engagement would have to be His rules, and eventually, all of Creation, including science, art, and all of the attending disciplines, would have to attest, wouldn't they? And didn't the Bible say somewhere that the very hills and rocks would cry out that He was God?

These were all bits and pieces of learning that took place over so many years, but they all started here in this little Methodist church with the beautiful arch and table imprinted with invitations to investigate the wonders of Creation and God and to worship Him in the beauty of holiness.

The amazing thing about all of this was yet to be understood. It yet remained to be seen that music embodied all of this search. Jana's love for music was awakened at this precise juncture and every new aspect of her musical understanding only deepened her eventual knowing that herein lay the answers—that music and its component parts held all the mysteries of life and Creation. She did not understand this for many years to come, but the seed was sown and would begin to grow to full fruition.

The counterpoints to the preexisting melody were being written daily.

Chapter 19

CANTARE

Critics said the summer of 1973 was a pinnacle year for the Festival of Two Worlds—a year to be written about in the annals of music for future musicians to muse over. What made it a pinnacle year for Jana was something even deeper and more commanding than the particular musical events and association with great musicians. For her it was the growing awareness that she was formulating her own philosophy of music, her sense that music occupied a place of universal, maybe even cosmic, proportions in the overarching scheme of things. She could not yet articulate this. Perhaps others had not, either, although strains of it were certainly in the air. For example, as Jana's son pointed out decades later, in *The Silmarillion,* J.R.R. Tolkien divined a theme similar to her own thoughts when he wrote about the Music of the Ainur, the Holy Ones who were conscripted by Iluvatar to sing, and as they sang they also listened and as they listened they also began to understand their ability to increase in unity and harmony. And they became, as it were, co-creators.

Their god, Iluvatar, taught them that in singing their Great Music together, they would be able to create great beauty through their harmonies. The dwelling places of Iluvatar were filled with great beauty and harmony and when this beautiful music went out into the void that was all around, it no longer was void, and so it seemed that Ainulindale and all that was contained in it was being sung into being by the harmonies of the music of the Ainur. Such was the myth of Iluvatar and the Ainur as it was all created by music and singing.

Jana was delighted and amazed by the imaginings of Tolkien.

And then there were *The Chronicles of Narnia*, written by C. S. Lewis. The book, *The Magicians Nephew*, was apparently the sixth book in the cycle begun about 1951. Digory Kirke and Polly Plummer were neighbors who found a secret tunnel connecting their homes. Through this tunnel they could access the netherworlds, one of which was the Land of Narnia. And it was here that they first met the great lion, Aslan. And here they are allowed to experience the very *Song of the Creation of Narnia*, as sung by Aslan. In C. S. Lewis' words:

> *"This is the gateway to many different kinds of worlds, from the desolate Charn where Queen Jadis once ruled through fear and cruelty, to a world not yet created. It is here that Digory and Polly meet Aslan for the first time and Aslan begins the wonderful song of creation which brings about the dawn of the first day in Narnia."*

It occurred to Jana that there was some sort of intrigue in the similarities of the fantasies of these two literary giants. They wrote in differ-

ent venues and with much different styles, and yet, their excursions into fantasy were so much alike. Where had the idea of *singing Creation into being* come from?

While she was in Italy, Jana began in earnest to explore the reality behind this beloved music which was life to her. And she was deeply intrigued by the realization that other people had already considered the possibility of a musical connection with the act of creation. As a spiritually and religiously oriented person, it seemed to her that music must have at its roots something eternal. Yet to pursue this thought, she had to discard or circumvent notions about music framed by ages of tradition, ritual, and practice. They did not satisfactorily answer her questions about the origins of this phenomenon that had such an intense impact on her life.

The scholastic year between Jana's first and second trips to Spoleto was a time of revelation on this topic, inspired in part by one of her teachers, Frances Poe. She was a diminutive woman with black hair which she wore quite short and absolutely straight, with smiling dark eyes, and a pixie-ish presence accentuated by the way she dressed. Although she was quiet and controlled in class, she always seemed just shy of a giggle. What animated her was the music of antiquity and the early Renaissance.

"Alright, class. The assignment for next Tuesday will require six hours of listening. The assigned work is *La Messe de Nostre Dame* by Guillaume de Machaut. You will listen for at least two hours before you start to analyze the rhythmic disposition of the work. Your responsibility also will be to provide me with a logical detailed analysis of the thematic materials and their various sources, and be able to support what you find."

No wonder she seemed just shy of a giggle. How in the world could a class of nineteen- or twenty-year-olds live up to an assignment like that? Most of them had probably never heard of a 12th century mass. Even though Jana enjoyed the status of being a more mature student than the others, her advanced years were no help in understanding these new musical challenges.

At first it was easy to dismiss early music and vow to dislike it for its harmonic and rhythmic sterility. Yet Francis Poe's enthusiasm and intense love for these vernal beginnings of tonal, diatonic music was contagious. So her students sat in the library cubicles for six hours over a week's duration and listened and listened and listened. They learned to deal with terms like talea, anacrustic, and non-isorhythmic. Even though there were no tempo markings or note values that were familiar to the students, the rhythm of that beautiful mass, *La Messe de Nostre Dame*, was hard to define but nonetheless permeated one's head and seemed right, like the sunrise and sunset, in harmony with the other rhythms of the universe. At that point in time, it was hard to define what was really going on in Jana's head.

For Jana, the assignment led to finding a new love—the music of antiquity. It spoke to her in an astonishing way. Its basic and primitive expressiveness seemed more truthful than she expected it to be. Had she expected truth from music? And what did that mean? This became still another question that would haunt her.

One day, apropos of nothing, Miss Poe challenged the class with something that had long intrigued Jana: "Where did music come from?" She posed the question in a way that suggested it was a weighty matter. The class responded with many answers, some profound, some naïve, some witty, but none seemed satisfying enough for Jana to put in her journal. Then Miss Poe leaned on the corner of the desk, sat back a bit and, bending her knee, lifted her left foot off the floor—a posture she always assumed when she was about to say something important—even though an impish twinkle belied her seriousness.

"Curt Sachs—you all remember who he was…" She referred to the famous German musicologist of the late 19th and early 20th centuries whose teachings about ancient music probably eclipsed all other writers of his time and ours. "In his book, *The Rise of Music in the Ancient World, East and West*, he made a profound observation: 'However far back we trace mankind, we fail to see the springing up of music.'"

"On the face of it," Miss Poe continued, "this seems like a bland statement of simple fact. But if you ponder the idea, I think you will be amazed that this can be interpreted to mean that music has *always* been present. The Bible mentions Jubal in Genesis 4:21 as the inventor of the harp and organ. This is no theology lesson, but that doesn't say Jubal invented music; rather, it seems reasonable to me that his inventions only made music more accessible. Some of you might say we can't use the Bible as a touchstone, since we don't know whether parts of it are fact or fiction. At any rate, Sachs seems to think, as I do, that 'however far back' we go, we still have no answer to where music started. That, my dear students, is the whole point. We do not know, do we?"

"Class dismissed!"

Following classes touched on rather detailed analyses of the codifying of the Psalms by King David, about 1000 B.C., according to references to historians such as Josephus; the early development of Ambrosian chant in Milan around A.D. 340 to 397; and the re-codifying of liturgical music by Pope Gregory in A.D. 590.

Jana, who had her own thoughts about the Bible, was not at all convinced that "we do not know" was the right conclusion about the beginnings of music, whatever Miss Poe or others thought.

Chapter 20

ELISION: OVERLAPPING PATTERNS

This quest for the origins of music, though unanswered by greater thinkers than she or her professor, still hung in the air for Jana. Isn't it more likely, she wondered, that music accompanied the origin of humanity and perhaps the very creation of the universe?

She realized that this concept made her a maverick in the eyes of her colleagues. Although Dr. Flummerfelt warned her not to carry this notion too far, Jana, undeterred, decided that for her master's thesis she would pursue research on the origins of music and the possible theological or spiritual ramifications of her findings.

Meanwhile, another Westminster teacher splashed a vivid color onto the palate of Jana's thinking. To call Bill Dalglish colorful was a huge understatement. He made many of his own clothes and one of his favorites was a jade green vest that he usually wore with a multi-colored shirt, dark blue corduroys, and cowboy boots. He had a huge space between his upper front teeth. His curly wiry hair complemented his Van Gogh beard. He spoke with

a slight lisp and his uncontrolled breathy laugh turned inward instead of spilling outward.

Bill, as everyone called him, taught music history and theory with a panache that included philosophy, religion, and fun. He brought a fresh context to his students' approach to music. He was not shy about saying that music is as vital to human existence as sex. He stressed that people's need for music was not simply something to listen to or to perform, and that its parameters were not exclusively musical in the narrow sense of the term. For instance:

"Shakespeare," Bill said, "is a musical experience. His poetry is a complex tapestry of word choice, rhythm, and mollified vocalizations. To really read Shakespeare one must read aloud and taste the words and listen to their sonorities." He recited the following, from Scene I of *Merchant of Venice*:

> *The man that hath no music in himself,*
> *Nor is not moved with concord of sweet sounds,*
> *Is fit for treasons, stratagems and spoils;*
> *The motions of his spirit are dull as night*
> *And his affections dark as Erebus:*
> *Let no such man be trusted.*

"I would be no thuch man," Bill lisped. So he gave Jana a new thought, that the world of literature, like the world of music, does not stand alone. Rhythm, color, dance, motion in words, and the human spirit itself is in need of things musical if it is to be trusted and fulfilled.

Jana eagerly looked forward to the philosophical nuggets Bill injected into his lectures. Like pulling Shakespeare's wisdom on the dark spirit of the musically bereft man out of its literary context and infusing it into the musical minds of his students. Usually Bill left little opportunity for discussion at those luminous moments. Like shafts of light glinting off a lead crystal bauble, these moments were here now—and then gone! Yet those fragile shafts of intellectual light never left Jana's mind. As they accumulated, they eventually helped illuminate her own theory of music—its meaning, its origins, and its sanctity.

Chapter 21

THE SHAW YEARS: FINDING TRUTH IN MUSIC

"*D*on't wash them out with sound rather than fulfill them with silence.*"—Robert Shaw, July 1977

On a mundane level, Jana could summarize her life during this fourteen-year period as follows: Graduate school accomplished. Learned to fly. Employed full-time as choral director in a Jersey high school for a decade. Many studies and other enriching experiences.

In terms of what really stirred Jana, however, the riveting center of her life was the Robert Shaw workshops that she looked forward to every summer. In 1974 while Jana was still a student at Westminster, she came home from her classes one day to find her husband waiting for her with a whiskey sour, that ritual precursor of things of a problematic or momentous nature. Earle even had dinner on the stove as he told Jana there was something he wanted her to consider.

"Robert Shaw is coming to Westminster for a summer workshop and I think you ought to go. Don't answer yet," Earle said to keep her from inter-

rupting. "I know you were going to say you've been away from Kenny during the school year, that you've been away during the Italy festival and you can't afford to leave again. But that's nonsense. I can cook and wash and all the rest. You must enroll right away before the quota is filled. No more to be said."

What Earle had asked Jana to consider was another fait accompli. Jana enrolled and soon packed her station wagon to the hilt and headed for Princeton. It was a Sunday afternoon, with the first rehearsal scheduled after dinner that night. What would the famed Robert Shaw be like?

Shaw was a stocky man with piercing eyes and a shock of unruly hair that hung damply in his face. He did not merely perspire, he sweated profusely, so much so that he wore a navy-blue towel around his neck and shoulders at all times. Navy blue to match the navy blue chinos and shirt that were his uniform.

"The Bible never gives up all of its secrets," Shaw said with a little chuckle, rocking from foot to foot with his shoulders just slightly hunched, "and neither does a great choral work. Never forget that."

Over the next fourteen years Jana would sing every summer for two weeks with Shaw and this group of fine musicians from all over the fifty states and a few foreign countries. No matter what works were sung, the thrill was the same. When Shaw did the same work a second or third time, he never failed to bring something new to it. His impact on Jana's thinking and imagination led eventually to the formulation of her own theories about music.

While Westminster teachers had opened new horizons for Jana, this experience with the greatest choral conductor eclipsed everything. In her second and third years with the master, Jana felt as if it were the first time. To sit under his baton was to learn theory, vocal and conducting technique, elocution, philosophy, and religion all at once. And to learn there is "truth in music," although that truth remained unfathomable. When asked to define it, Shaw, with an enigmatic smile would say, "God only knows—but get out of the way of the music. It is not about you, it is about the music." That was one of the great lessons he taught with so little effort, so few words.

"Remember," he would say, "make the first sound right, because once you have let it go into the cosmos, it will never stop. Eternity is a long time." And he would chuckle his sly chuckle.

Another of Shaw's favorite lecture subjects was the functionality of words. "The meaning of words should not be limited or reduced to their dictionary equivalents," he said. This concept stuck in Jana's memory bank. Some fifty years later, when she was studying Hebrew and struggling with the search for truth, it was helpful to remember that words have far-flung lives beyond their common everyday meanings. Shaw's philosophy of communication became a veritable treasure house of expressive thought and information.

After one monstrous rehearsal full of problems and unresolved vocal issues, he wrote the following poem in a letter to his choir members:

> *Half-ideas are transient-shaped,*
> *Or else they must dissolve somehow each into each,*
> *If only they would stand completely still*
> *Until one found the words their size.*
> *"I see, your measurements are thus and thus—*

That's clear enough."

You inventory your entire stock—

"Now this should fit"—and turn to find

It really doesn't fit at all.

You have a cubed suit for a sphered thought.

You were sure that thought had corners!

When the workshop performed Bach's *B minor Mass*, Shaw opened the first rehearsal with one of his most profound lectures, asking, "What is art? Or, translated, what is music? The arts," he continued, "tell us something about the nature of man—more than any other discipline. Organizations of church and state do not communicate this so completely. The arts tell us something about the nature of mystery and divinity, of God."

Shaw taught more by the questions he asked than by the answers he gave. In the opening bars of the Kyrie of the Bach *Mass*, he drew attention to the juxtaposition of the ascending and descending minor seconds in the melodic line. He adjured the choir to pay very close attention to them, because they may have some mysterious meaning connected to the cry for mercy:

"Why do you think Bach repeated over and over this tiny figure of the descending minor second? Maybe the Greeks had something? Maybe their understanding of the communicative power of music was not too far afield. Plato and Aristotle seemed to think there was some mysterious way in which music could make man one thing or the other just by its sounds. This pleading minor second sure as anything makes you understand that man needs mercy. Then it turns right around and is heard ascending—salvation. Hmmmm." And then, his little two-footed shuffle and chuckle.

Shaw's grasp of the Gloria was extraordinary. "'Glory be to God on high, and on earth peace to men of good will.' In triple meter? Triple meter is eccentric—it's lopsided. Like our human attempts to praise almighty God?"

It would take Jana pages and pages to recount the myriad lessons gleaned from that one work. In fact, every work learned under Robert Shaw's baton revealed the awesome understanding this man had, not only of the music, but of its timeless and incomprehensible mysteries. But he never explained what he meant by *truth in music*. Perhaps because of the inscrutableness of the concept? Or was it something yet to be revealed? Jana wondered.

Chapter 22

CREDO: I BELIEVE

$\mathcal{S}$inging Beethoven's *Missa Solemnis* with Shaw was another marvelous experience for Jana. During two performances within the span of several years, she noted many differences in interpretation, but yet with a cohesiveness in approach. One message, but expressed in various ways. Jana felt there were no words to match the depth of spiritual perception sensed by singing a work like this. This made her realize that many issues in God's scheme of things cannot be explained but nevertheless must be acknowledged and ultimately understood on intuitive and spiritual levels. Shaw seemed uniquely in touch with the unknowable, and completely at ease with accepting the mysteries of life, things that can only be grasped by *not* knowing. Life is characterized by "fracture, abstraction, the unknowable God—and silence," he said during one rehearsal.

Before the choir started to sing, Shaw described Beethoven's monumental work, as recorded in Jana's notes: "This work is written in cut time—two beats to the measure—half notes getting one beat. Never mind. It doesn't start on the second beat! You will look at the score and disagree with me.

Listen! Silence! The first beat is very strong, but the first sound doesn't happen until the second beat. Interesting. It does not start on the up-beat. It starts *in silence*. Strong silence. God is not available to man in the first expression of the Kyrie. Its dynamics are square. There is no relationship between forte and piano, no transition from loud to soft. It is fractured and frightening. The whole piece argues with itself. Melody contradicts harmony and text. There is a juxtaposition of being inside and outside of God. Poor man. At the end of the Kyrie there is no hope. Then there is a quickening tempo in the Christe. There is hope. Christ is available to man. There is comfort in the motive, that is, in the melodic lines of the voices. There are fractures, but there is grace. Again, silence is an integral part of this movement."

"I am always humbled by that silence," Shaw continued. "This magnificent work at one and the same time deals with the Almighty, the Omnipotent, and humanity. What a contrast. It is the schizophrenia between grace and chaos. You can relate to it in one of two ways—either with nothing to impinge, and that would be insanity, or you can open yourself to every facet of the work and try to make it fit together. Consider the greatness of the mind of Beethoven, an unecclesiastical person, coming so close to Christian principles. Extraordinary!"

Throughout preparations for performing the *Missa*, Shaw's sense of the holy was overriding, laying the very foundation for musical interpretation. Hence, he was meticulous about vocal production and sound, admonishing the choir that, since choral music was a spiritual thing, to do a little less singing and a little more listening.

The Gloria in the *Missa* was, true to its name, glorious.

"People," that was Shaw's favorite name for his singers. "People, this Gloria is a kaleidoscopic change in direction and qualities of motion.

It may not work unless we are ecstatic. Sing the word 'gloria' as if you were running into a brick wall. Listen! You can't manufacture music out of yourself. Let the trombones come in first and then push them off the stage with your sound." But then at one point he said, "You are singing so loud nobody can hear the music."

In the beginning of the Gloria he portrayed a vivid insight into the Qui Tollis, which is interpreted, "Thou takest away the sins of the world, have mercy upon us, receive our prayer." Man is pleading to God, but Shaw urged the choir to realize that man is pleading because "the situation is that the world *is* sinful." Interestingly, one of Shaw's favorite pieces of advice was to "allow every note, every word, every phrase to have its own is-ness."

The last movement of the *Missa* was transcendental to Jana. The imagery of the warfare between good and evil, the fracturing of warfare on the spiritual level, the renewal of hope in the Dona Nobis, and the utterance of just one more prayer, Pacem, and one more hope, Dona Pacem, Pacem, left her breathless and exhausted physically but exhilarated spiritually and musically.

But, above all, the Crucifixus and the Et Resurrexit in the Credo became defining moments in Jana's quest for truth—for truth in music and in spirit. Shaw explained them this way:

"People, in the Adagio, we will experience instant nails. The hammer stroke is unmitigated and irrefutable. It strikes on the last 32nd beat of measure 156 and rebounds on the held note in the beginning of measure 157. DA-aaah, DA-aaah, DA-aaah, over and over again to measure 162."

"The Allegro, on the other hand, is flat-footed resurrection, instantaneously in root position. A whirlwind reinforced by the Credo theme.

People, this is ecstasy, speaking in tongues, hysteria. Transported emotional music. Not a question of vocalism. It's a question of musical honor. Looking forward to the resurrection of the dead and the life of the world to come. Intimations of immortality. Quiet, as if only in the mind of God."

Jana was transported by the explanation and by the way it informed the choir's performance.

Shaw's "people" were a motley bunch of musicians, Christian, Jewish, believer, non-believer, conservative, liberal, theistic, atheistic. For all of them, Shaw's incisive lectures triggered the unrelenting quandaries: What is music? Where were its ultimate beginnings? What does music communicate? How does it communicate?

Years later Jana happened upon a Cambridge University scholar, Jeremy S. Begbie, who posed these very same questions in his exploration, *Theology, Music and Time*. "It is clear," Begbie wrote, "that music is one of the most powerful communicative media we have, but *how* it communicates and *what* it communicates are anything but clear."

To Jana, it became exquisitely clear that the unresolved issue churning inside her was not whether there is truth in music, but rather what *is* that truth.

Chapter 23

MELODIC DOUBLING: UNCHAINED MELODY

ll the moments of epiphany, all the experiences of high emotional stimulation that were the hallmark of Jana's three years at Westminster, need not be recounted. But to better understand her intellectual journey, it is important to look at the performance phenomena that constantly accompanied her purely academic work.

It was mandatory for every student from sophomore to graduate level to sing in the Symphonic Choir with its average size of 250 to 300 singers. Each semester this choir sang in at least one of the famous East Coast concert halls, a custom established by John Finlay Williamson, the school's founder. Great choral music, he believed, needed to be experienced at the highest level to be understood correctly, so he saw to it that his beloved students had this exposure. This tradition, though somewhat elitist, survived decades of change in educational philosophies and is still followed.

After rehearsing for most of each semester, the crowning glory for Jana was to sing under men such as Leonard Bernstein, Antol Dorati, Pierre

Boulez, William Steinberg, and Michael Tilson Thomas, and the magnificent orchestras they commanded, the New York Philharmonic, the Na-
tional Symphony Orchestra, and the Pittsburgh Symphony. The works
sung covered almost four hundred years of choral writing, from Bach to
Kodaly and Bernstein. The range of styles was incredible, so different
for Bach's *B minor Mass*, Haydn's *Harmoniemesse*, Mozart's *Requiem*,
Bruckner's *Te Deum*, Verdi's *Te Deum* and his great *Requiem*, Kodaly's
Psalmus Hungaricus, and Bernstein's *Chichester Psalms*.

This vast panoply of human creativity was another wonder to Jana.
How could this Western music system give voice to so much varied
emotion, whether joyous or full of pathos? How could seven notes on
a staff expand to produce a repertory that was virtually unfathomable?
How could so many different human beings with such differing life
experiences in such differing time sectors create such beauty on such
vastly differing levels? Her mind turned to her childhood teachings of
the Creative God and to the science teacher who said every snowflake
was different and that every rose had its own peculiar beauty. Nothing
in nature was exactly alike, even the most insignificant thing has its own
individuality. Despite that, there is overwhelming evidence of universal
cohesiveness. Without this order and unity, Jana mused, the entire gal-
axy might collapse.

Finally at the end of her Westminster journey, Jana stood waiting to
process into the Princeton University Chapel for graduation. Someone
brought her a program and pointed to her name on the back page where
the graduates were listed. There were two stars by her name—*magna
cum laude!* Her husband, sitting in the audience, could hear Jana yell.

"Do you mean to tell me you didn't know you were magna cum
laude?" Earle asked her later.

94

"No, I was too busy just learning all I could," she answered. "Well, anyhow, I wonder how far that honor will get me?"

She had little time to wonder. The state of New Jersey at that time had just mandated that schools hire ancillary music and art teachers for mainstreamed mentally and neurologically challenged students. The head of the music department in the town of Freehold had heard about Jana and phoned her. "Would you accept a part-time position as music teacher for the TMRs?"

TMRs were trainable mentally retarded, as certain mentally challenged students were called. The job would be one or two classes a day for three days a week for the coming semester, with the possibility of turning into a full-time position afterwards. Which it did.

Teaching the mentally challenged was a challenge for Jana. Not trained to work with retarded children, she knew little about their so-called incapabilities. She did not know they were assumed to be incapable of learning to sing in tune. She did not presume that their difficulties with academic learning meant that, therefore, they could not succeed at other kinds of learning, especially musical learning. She could not accept the typical notion that Down syndrome children could not possibly have real talent. She soon found it obvious that they *did* have talent and Jana covenanted with herself to disprove the common acceptance of their inherent inabilities.

She found support in this from a book on musical therapy in special education, whose author wrote, "The idea that the brain-injured or mentally deficient have a 'primitive' consciousness and that the music used with them should be on a primitive level negates the whole potential of music therapy."

Music therapy was a rising discipline in the 1970s and it literally struck a chord with Jana. She became good friends with Bill Shoppell, supervisor of the choral music department. In the months and years ahead, he gave Jana a great deal of latitude to pursue what she wanted to accomplish at Freehold Township High School.

That part-time position with the "trainables" turned into a full-time position as Director of Choral Music at Freehold High School the following fall. Jana took over the entire choral music department, including the four-year high school choir program in addition to the music program for the TMRs who soon became her first love. Music had a tremendous impact on them and it was a joy for her to watch their progress.

In addition to the work with the TMRs, her first major undertaking with the mainstream high school program was producing Benjamin Britten's one-act opera, *Noye's Fludde*. One of the students was the son of the famous Metropolitan Opera bass, Paul Plishka. Young Paul had a magnificent voice, much like his father's, with a low C that resonated unlike anything a 16-year-old would be expected to produce. A young soprano, Livia Polise, had a unique voice with a depth of color and trueness of pitch that also belied her young years. With solo voices like these, Jana could not resist the temptation to mount this story of Noah's ark for the community's enjoyment. She had an intuitive compulsion to bring a real, operatic experience to these kids who basically knew only pop and rock music and had little, if any in some cases, notion of the true beauty of an opera, of all things. Amazingly, it worked.

The parents were enthusiastic and even helped Jana to get 128 seventh and eighth graders from the junior high school to create an impressive menagerie for the ark when it was finally built. A local news reporter wrote the review later with humorous clarity:

"Mrs. Hutchison went to the middle school to get 128 animals for the ark!"

Two weeks before production, nothing seemed to be working. The senior Paul Plishka urged Jana not to panic, saying, "We get used to this at the Met. Just think of it as controlled chaos."

In the midst of the confusion, Jana had to go to a music educators' convention in Atlantic City. On the long drive from Freehold, a fierce thunder storm swept in off the ocean, turning the air black. The wind was so strong Jana had to hang onto the steering wheel for all she was worth. Thunder roared, lightning shattered the sky, and volumes of rain poured out. As quickly as the storm arrived, it breathed its last gasp and disappeared. The sun was low in the western sky and suddenly a double rainbow arched across the Jersey pinelands and dipped both ends down into the sea. Not one, but two perfect rainbows. Jana stopped the car, awed by the sight. Her thoughts tumbled: "God sent one rainbow to Noah. He has sent me two. I'll accept this as a promise, Lord, that the chaos will be controlled."

At dress rehearsal, which was open to the entire school district, chaos had not lessened much, but accepting it made it bearable. The first glitch came as the 128 little animals were marching down the auditorium aisles joyously singing "Kyrie eleison" in measured repetition as they approached the ark on the stage. But once on stage they had no place to go because Mr. Noye (Noah) found the door to the ark was stuck. Jana, herself thunderstruck now, hissed at Lynn Beach, the concert mistress, "What do we do now?!" Lynn whispered calmly, "Keep Kyrie-ing till they get the door open." It worked.

That crisis passed and it was time for the flood-storm to commence. The industrial arts teacher had given the stage hands a large piece of sheet

metal to rattle for thunder. But Jeff Plishka, Paul's younger son who lived in his own little world, was distressed that there was no lightning. With a sudden inspiration he scurried to the lighting panel and began rapidly flicking the mercury light switch up and down. The strobe effect was marvelous. Except that it made it impossible for the orchestra members to read their music. Lynn again to the rescue told Jana, "Get Jeff away from that light panel," which she did and another calamity was averted. It seemed as if the promise of the twin rainbows held. The opening performance and the three that followed were gratifyingly successful.

This experience proved to Jana that musical beauty and understanding is available to everyone. The necessary ingredient is exposure, lovingly administered. She was encouraged to try more ambitious events. Obviously, music had power.

In ensuing years Jana brought *Amahl and the Night Visitors* and *H.M.S. Pinafore* to the Freehold High stage. She also started a madrigal choir, an auditioned group that became popular in the area as it introduced people to the 14th and 15th century music that Frances Poe had taught Jana to love. Many decades later some of Jana's former students told her that their choral music experiences with her had changed their lives in many ways. This power of music to inspire people to higher aspirations was the very mystery Jana was trying to decipher.

There was a growing ground swell to completely secularize music education, and this secularization only served to make Jana's ideas about the eternal inferences in the art of music more and more remote and difficult to discuss with any of her peers.

But somehow, that kind of secular reasoning did not fit with other developing theories such as music therapy, for example. Medicine was beginning to take seriously the idea that music could and *did* aid in the

98

healing process, especially in the area of mental health. What could music possibly have to do with the health of the human mind if it were not of some significant worth beyond the veil of human understanding? And what about those tremors of sympathetic vibration when the human organism heard or intuited beauty in a musical sound? Individual, personal harmonics responding to the particular vibrations of a particular musical sound? What was it? Did the human body—the human spirit—have harmonic resonances like a crystal glass?

The further along the way that Jana traveled, the more convinced she became that there was a dimension that neither she nor anyone else yet understood about this thing called music.

Dr. Rosalie Pratt, one of Jana's graduate professors, greatly influenced her in seeing music as a healing art. Dr. Pratt introduced her to the Orff-Kodaly and Dalcroze methodologies and urged her to experiment with them for her mentally challenged students. The results were not too far shy of miraculous. Students who could hardly speak were singing. Some who merely sat on the floor rocking began to bang on xylophones and eventually to actually play them. Several who loved to dance and move around learned to read music on a huge painter's drop cloth with the music staff taped on it. After two years, the TMRs were playing in a small xylophone orchestra with rhythm sticks and drums. There seemed no rational explanation beyond that of the healing power of music.

Part 2

DEVELOPMENT
The Beauty of Holiness

Chapter 24

PARODY MASS: A DECLINING PHILOSOPHY

While the power of music had become increasingly apparent to Jana, she was unable to pinpoint what the mechanics of that power were. Maybe mechanics was not the right word. She knew almost all musicians gave homage to this power but up to this point, she could not define it or name its source in a way that would be definitive enough to "stand up in court."

There was an academic philosophy that became very popular about the time that Jana was in grad school and it annoyed Jana to no end. She felt she stood alone in her opposition to it. Her spirit was offended by it. This philosophy was touted by some of the leading educators of the day like Charles R. Hoffer and Leonard B. Meyer. One of the rationales for the need for music and the arts in the school curriculum was the idea that the purpose of music was to "better fill one's leisure hours" or "to enhance the quality of human life." This may be true but Jana knew instinctively that there was something deeper, much deeper, than that as a *raison d'etre* of music and the arts. The thinking behind this shallow and ill-thought-out philosophy, Jana felt, pro-

vided plenty of justification for the individuation of musical taste which was burgeoning in this era. The idea that good music was whatever anyone chose to declare, free of any rules, boundaries, or values, struck Jana as a blow against truth in music—even though, at that point, she could not herself define that truth.

So she struggled to find her way through the maze of contradictory philosophies. The texts she was forced to study seemed to center the creative act on the talent of the *person*, without questioning the source of such talent. This led to an explanation effectively segregating society into the uniquely gifted and almost all the rest who were considered untalented. If that were so, Jana wondered, why were there such a multitude of excellent singers in the 15th and 16th centuries? Where did Bach find all those sopranos with fluid voices who could not only manage, but adeptly perform, his *Coffee Cantata*?

Curiosity and imagination, hallmarks of her personality, would not let Jana stop pursuing these questions. They forced her to try to come to grips with her sense that, for her, the *real* realities in life were in the arts. Was this due in part to her father's ever-failing health or her mother's depression—things a growing child could not cope with? Was it not easier to sit at the piano and let her aching soul find healing there? That felt real. The ineffable presence of a Bach chorale, the beauty of a Bouvier-de-Cachard painting hanging in the window of a Princeton gallery, or the exquisite balance of Michelangelo's *David* in Florence, Italy—these were the realities easily seen and heard when she was no longer a child. How did these realities relate to the stars of the heavens and to the superficial and often contradictory teachings she received about their meanings? Jana found no clear way to reconcile the complex issues of art, theology, philosophy, and science. Until, that is, she came into contact with Pythagoras.

Edward Rothstein, a mathematician turned musician, in 1982 wrote a *New York Times* article, Math and Music: The Deeper Links—How Two Abstract Systems Reshape Our Understanding of Reality.[ii] Jana's mind went into fast forward as she read this article about the golden ratio. It told of Pythagoras' belief that all music was the "expression of number in sound," and that Aristotle "supposed the whole heaven to be a harmonia and a number."

The musical harmony of the early Pythagoreans was constructed solely by manipulating the first four integers. They discovered that consistent "pleasing" musical intervals were generated by dividing a vibrating string in ratios formed by these four numbers. The ratio 1 to 2 yields an octave; 3 to 2 yields the fifth, and 4 to 3 yields the fourth, thus establishing the first set of manageable harmonies. Over the last 2,600 years Pythagorean philosophy has phased in and out of favor, but it is still basically accepted as the beginning of musical theory.

Pythagoras' work with the golden ratio gave rise to explorations of this *Divina Proportione* by scholars in virtually every discipline: mathematics, of course, plus aesthetics, architecture, art, sculpture, natural science, and music. Even historians and philosophers, too, who defined the golden mean as the "felicitous middle between two extremes, one of excess and one of deficiency."

Jana took note that all this interest in an abstract thought was generated by hundreds of intellectual giants in differing disciplines over thousands of years. Even in the world of literature and folk lore—from Genesis to the Silmarillion to Narnia—every culture seemed to have fantasies about the power and origins of music and creation. Jana felt it

---

[ii] *Math and Music: The Deeper Links:* New York Times: Edward Rothstein: August 29, 1982

was unlikely that there were no absolutes behind these common theories and legends.

On a professional level, Jana often felt caught between her ideals of teaching music and the academic myopia of top administrators. A prime example of her clash with bureaucracy concerned Liva Polise who had sung the role of Mrs. Noye. A year or so after that production, brilliant Livia completed most of her graduation credits though she was only a junior in high school. Jana designed an independent study for her so she could stay in high school until her sixteenth birthday. The administration would not authorize this. At the same time, administrators accused Jana of proselytizing because of a choral mass she taught the madrigal choir, leading her to sense that her values of beauty and spiritual oneness were being violated. As pressures for her resignation escalated, she found herself in the office of Victor Crespy, the district school superintendent, to argue her case.

"Vic, I can't understand you or the board," she said. "How can a special student like Livia be perceived as outside the parameters of public education? We should provide opportunity for all special students. You do it for TMRs, so why not the gifted? I can do it if you give me a chance." This was some years before curricula for the gifted became common practice.

"And opposition to singing a mass is pure idiocy. How can people accuse me of proselytizing when I am sharing a work of beauty with children who have little enough of it in their lives? We didn't even translate the text. I taught the mass purely as a work of art."

She paused while Vic and her immediate supervisor, Bill Shoppell, tried to shake off their shock at her sharp words. Then she continued: "I

Chapter 24

thought you, the academic hierarchy, were here for the good of the students. Obviously you're not."

Jana turned on her heel and left the office. Shortly after this outburst, she resigned the teaching position that had become so much a part of her identity. Years would pass before Jana realized that Vic and Bill were doing their best and were literally in an untenable position, caught between a fine teacher and the Board of Education. For many years, it would be a hallmark of her professional life to be misunderstood, because her thinking and her passions ran so deep.

Chapter 25

TACET

The frustration of professional misunderstanding hurt Jana more deeply than she realized at the time. Her passion for things she most believed in had cost her the participation in and acceptance in the field of endeavor that was her life's blood. It caused her to abandon almost anything of a musical nature, as if that meant nothing to her. Instead, she turned to flying, which she had started to learn while still teaching at Freehold.

Still married to Earle, Jana's flying became a divisive force adding to the growing stress in their marriage. She would stay over weekends with her fellow student pilot, Bonnie, who had been a close friend for several years. Earle did not enjoy that Jana was often away from Lavallette and Bonnie was outspoken about him. "When are you going to wake up and see that your marriage is not working? Earle, besides being 17 years older than you, is a recluse and is dragging you down. The older he gets, the worse it will be."

"He is such a good man," Jana countered. "He took care of my children when I was down and out. He paved the way for my education. He kept my

son while I was in school and for all the years I traipsed around to Spoleto. I can't just leave him."

"If he is such a good man and if he knew how much you need to break away from his isolated life, would he wish to keep you in misery? He probably doesn't realize how much he is keeping you from doing what you love."

This was pilot talk. Actually, Bonnie had no insight into the other Jana, the person forever grateful to Earle for giving her the opportunity to enjoy and expand her musical gifts far beyond what she could have dreamed. Yet this talk with Bonnie led to a conversation that ultimately ended the marriage—a conversation Jana would never forget.

Jana had been flying and came home late. "Earle," she said, "I can't go on like this. You have been so good to me, but I have known for a long time that I can't give you what you really need. I wonder whether even you know what is good for you. Therapy hasn't helped. Neither has counseling…"

She stopped in mid-sentence, recalling the day they had gone for marriage counseling. The psychiatrist asked Earle why he had married Jana. His answer that lodged in Jana's brain was that he married her because she was a social asset.

"…I don't think anything can help," she continued softly after this recollection. "I don't know what lies ahead but I have to keep seeking my own Holy Grail. You seem unable to give me the one thing I most need—love—without trying to change me. I think it is hopeless."

The divorce was painful for both of them. They were not adversaries, just locked in two opposite worlds: one of insatiable striving, one of scholarly complacency. Fortunately, time would allow them to become friends again.

Jana reveled in her new flying skill. By 1984 she had attained her instrument instructor's rating. This meant she could teach others to fly in the clouds with no reference to the ground whatsoever. The work brought her into contact with a new and largely male society. The novelty of being the only female instructor at the airport was exhilarating, a narcotic of sorts that took the edge off her hurt over the experience at Freehold and her divorce from Earle.

Life took on a different hue after her divorce and move to Robbinsville, New Jersey, near the airport. The grand piano she kept was one of the few links to her past, to the voice lessons, recitals, singing in great concert halls with the greatest conductors, teaching, and conducting. She hardly mentioned such things to her new cohorts. How could she discuss the beauty of Debussy with a bunch of self-centered pilots of the male gender?

Five summers passed after she left Earle. These years were fraught with surviving financially. Flight instructors made only a few dollars an hour and commission sales were few and irregular. Outside sales and a head-hunting job for a major executive search firm in Princeton helped. Yet, whatever else she was doing, one thing remained unchanged. Every summer during that painful period Jana would take two weeks off to sing in the Robert Shaw workshop at her alma mater, Westminster Choir College.

Chapter 26

LIBERA ME

A s Shaw mounted the podium at opening rehearsals each year, his "people" would wait eagerly to hear what pearls of wisdom—musical, philosophical, or theological—he would grace them with. The last year Jana sang with Shaw, 1987, was a cardinal year. Perhaps the master was sensing his own mortality, or maybe the imminent mortality of great choral art, or possibly both. In any event, that year was without question a life-changing year for Jana.

"First of all, people, let me say this. Your responsibility as choral directors is to create an atmosphere where your musicians are not embarrassed for caring. Professionalism puts as great a strain on music as it does on sex." He was urging the choir not to lose its spontaneity. Yet he posed a contrasting message as he continued:

"We live in an intellectually impoverished society, so it is our responsibility as choral conductors to restore as much reason as we can. Our sacred music deals in matters of holiness. Since holiness has to do with intellectuality, an

intellectually impoverished society cannot hope to be holy. Don't forget that we rarely achieve the perfection we strive for. We never quite get to the place that we can ask the dove to descend. Only God can do that."

After the choir ventured the first bit of sight reading that evening, Shaw shouted, "Requiem! But not one word. Three syllables! Three! RE-QUI-EM! Split the atom! Look into its insides. What if this RE-QUI-EM was the whole piece?" The choir partly understood, but why split the atom?

Chapter 27

ALEATORY SINGING: INDETERMINACY

*J*ana had reached a critical point in her life. She was lonely but afraid to venture into another serious relationship. Her beloved music had gone begging. She was accustomed to droughts when she was unable to embrace her music. It did not escape her that she probably brought these droughts on herself by some of the poor choices she was wont to make. Too, she was feeling a sense of resignation about music as a career—getting older, her opportunities for further success seemed remote.

Of course Jana could not ignore the fact that she had had a lifetime of exceptional experiences because she chose mostly "the road not traveled by," and, therefore, she had journeyed to places both real and aesthetic that few people of her age and status could even imagine. Yet she was tired and wanted to be freed from the "not knowing," from the constant queries that swirled around in her mind.

"What is the real truth behind the music I love so much and why can't other people understand what it is that I hear and see and what is so important about it all anyway?"

Maybe if she just left it all behind. Maybe if she just made herself stop thinking about the beauty which she could not absorb or delineate. No more hours of study and practice. No more auditions for herself or her students. Relief from the competition. Relief from stultifying administrators who suppressed creativity. These notions were on the positive side.

On the negative side at this period was Jana's feeling of alienation from her church, which was sad and strange because, if one had asked her about it, she would have said the church was at the very core of her being. And, somehow, she knew that the truth in music and the truth in faith were intrinsic, one to the other.

Jana did make the long trip to Lavallette to play the church organ there, and Earle seemed to be able to accept the kind of friendship they had had before their marriage as being normal and maybe even good. But trying to pretend that nothing bad had happened was awkward and stressful for Jana. Perhaps it was easier for Earle who had become accustomed to maintaining a prolonged charade after his first divorce. Most of the time, however, Jana busied herself with flying and teaching flying. And thinking.

"Where am I really going and how am I going to know when I get there? Do I really want—do I really need—the excitement of this new life surrounded by airplanes and men who love to live on the edge of things? Does all of this give me the same satisfaction that conducting a Bach Cantata gives me? Where is the beauty of a well-turned phrase to be found in an airplane cockpit? And yet, I love to fly…"

116

Jana reflected on her life as a pilot—one of only three thousand or so women who could name "flight instructor" as one of their credentials in the 1970s and 1980s. She recalled her first flight student, one Ali Kabas, a bright young man from Istanbul who was studying physics at Princeton University. He was adventuresome and fun to fly with, but he had a great deal of trouble remembering that a large part of controlling the three-dimensional flight path of an aircraft was positive use of the rudder pedals. Especially when practicing stalls, with the nose pitched high and the airplane in a steep bank. On this particular day, Jana recalled, she had told Ali to climb up to five thousand feet for their stall training session.

"No need to taunt the muses who might try to throw us into the ground, Ali! Let's have plenty of air between us and the earth, just in case."

His dark eyes, almost black, sparked with fun and anticipation. He loved to fly, too, and was determined to get his private license before returning to Turkey so he could get into the Turkish Air Force. He always wore a heavy, almost Oriental cologne and on that hot July afternoon, the scent filled the tiny cockpit with a heady opaqueness. There was a definite air of some impending something, but Jana was familiar with that feeling; one never knew what a student pilot would do next and one always had to be prepared for the worst while hoping for the best, and had better be capable of orchestrating the best outcome, at that.

Ali was a fairly aggressive student, sure of himself, and without being arrogant, he exerted a positive approach to the things at hand. And so, up to five thousand feet the little Cessna climbed as Jana kept up a steady stream of instructions:

"Watch your air speed, Ali, full power in the climb and raise the nose to maintain at least 85 knots. Remember, in the climb under full power you need much more right rudder to keep the nose straight. Torque

and slip-stream keep trying to pull you to the left. Right rudder… right rudder…"

Finally, they leveled off and started preparations for the actual stalling exercise.

"O. K., Ali, power back to idle. Lift the nose to slow us down to 60 knots or so, right aileron into the turn. 30 degrees of bank…and RIGHT RUDDER, RIGHT RUDDER, RIGHT RUDDER!"

But it was too late. Jana knew it was too late. The stall snapped alive much too violently in that nose-high bank and Ali had neglected the right rudder. The high wing stalled with a vengeance and the little plane lurched over onto its back to the left. The nose fell abruptly and started to spin—which way?? Which way?? Ali had the controls locked back into his chest which only made the spin wind up faster and faster.

With a sudden hard "thwack" to his ribs with her elbow, Jana broke Ali's death grip on the yoke and the nose of the little Cessna started to seek its own equilibrium. A few more wobbles like a wounded duck and the spin was over. The startling awareness that made student and instructor both gasp was that they had lost over two-thousand feet in the process. How happy for them both that they started out at five-thousand feet instead of the prescribed fifteen-hundred!

When he knew he was safe, Ali grinned his big, handsome Turkish grin and said, "Do it again! Do it again!"

"No, no, no, Ali. We go home now!" Jana had just grown up as a flight instructor. But somehow, the beauty of that little airplane responding to the laws of physics which, like the laws of sound, are inviolable and each beautiful in its own right, reached into her very soul and made her feel once again, in a different way, the almost eternal awareness that

whatever laws there be, they are, indeed, inviolable because they are eternally conceived in the heart and mind of the Creator Himself and cannot be explained outside of the limits set by that Creator. No matter how far afield her life took her, Jana was still a consummate musician and a deeply religious individual, finding God in all the wondrous rhythms and harmonies of the universe. She had not really articulated this to herself until she was outside that cocoon—her church community—where things spiritual were rarely questioned or discussed but just taken for granted.

One fall night, combining business and pleasure, Jana was taking David Phillips, a commercial student, on a long cross-country training flight that had to be conducted after dark. They flew to Duchess County, north of New York City, so they could have dinner with Wink and Ray, Jana's sister and brother-in-law, who lived near the little Sky Park airport. After 9, when they were all back at the airport preparing for the flight home, Jana was awe struck by what she saw: "David! Wink! Ray! Look! Look!"

She was hardly coherent. The entire northern sky was a gossamer curtain of shimmering icy green waves of color that undulated back and forth and up and down, a heavenly tarantella. The waves curled and warped and spread until the entire sky was covered in green energy. They turned deep jade green, then disappeared into a thin white-green wash. Then the curling came back. Dark green pencil strokes outlined the dancing waves. Magnificent!

That familiar chill of unspoken emotion coursed through Jana's body. All four stood transfixed as the show waxed and waned for over ten minutes. Suddenly it was gone, as if it never happened.

"Well, David, we must go and you will have to do all the work flying home," Jana said. "I'm exhausted from all this beauty." She was not

making this up. The energy of that glorious display had reached into her soul, as if she were part of the dance, leaving her physically drained.

On the way home, David kept up a running description of the wonders of the aurora borealis. A graduate student in Princeton's physics department, he talked about "coronal mass ejections" and "long-duration MI solar flares." Jana finally could not bear it and surprised herself at the certainty with which she challenged him.

"David, science isn't everything. Can't you see that all nature sings? Even the rocks and mountains have songs to sing about creation. Don't you ever wonder what the aurora sounds like?"

Knowing David was a classical music enthusiast, she continued, "Can't you see that those magnificent rhythms and color transformations we just saw are as much an expression of beauty and emotion as any symphony ever composed? Don't you wonder what such creative energy comes from? What is it that music and art of all kinds are reflecting? Surely it goes back to the most primitive of times."

Apparently she did not succeed in getting through to David. They finished the flight in silence.

On another evening Jana was flying with her own instructor, headed south over the Jersey shoreline. The setting sun was poised on the rim of the horizon in a blaze of orange and coral red etched against the black outline of the land, with rays of gold reaching far up into the sky. This entire skyscape was duplicated, reflected in the glassy-smooth waters of Barnegat Bay.

"Take the controls, Ron. This is so beautiful I have to do something!" Jana literally could not concentrate on her instrument flying.

Before Ron could stop her, Jana unbuckled her seat belt, climbed over the seat and grabbed the camera in her flight bag. How often she thanked God that she was able to immortalize that moment. That photograph remains one of her prized possessions.

Such experiences reinforced Jana's sensitivity to the mysteries and interrelatedness of everything in the universe. They reminded her of Robert Shaw's frequent talk about that in rehearsals. Although never quite defining it in words, he kept trying to capture the concept in music. "Split the atom," Shaw yelled at the choir in the first measures of Verdi's Requiem. Indeed. And everything remained aleatory*—so much beauty and so much power in the whole of creation and no way to sufficiently explain it. Words were confusing; words could not express the beauty, and the morass of verbal attempts only caused more confusion. Somehow Shaw knew that sound and beauty and words and music had a dire, eternal need to be revealed—one to the other. "Split the atom!" What was this awesome energy that gnawed at Jana's intellect, demanding to be articulated?

---

* *See definition in Glossary on page 228*

Chapter 28

LIBERA ME: AGAIN

o, during this liberating time, without abandoning her quest to understand the source of music, Jana's tether lines became tenuous and left her with a deep sense of being alone in her thoughts and beliefs. That is, until a man, a pilot, came into her life. Jack was exactly that—the "man's man," she admitted to him, that she had always wanted—quiet, sure of himself and self-confident. His grandmother had told him as a child that he was perfect and he was happy to believe it, even into his sixties. A flight maven at the airport, he had flown B-24s in World War II. Younger pilots looked up to Jack with awe. He was a straight-thinking retired engineer who lived life logically by a checklist. Black was black and white was white.

Jana and Jack married and built a large log house on Smith Mountain Lake in rural west-central Virginia. Living in the hills provided lots of time for reflection and communing with nature. Jana liked to stand on the deck, face the hills across the cove, and sing a short made-up phrase or a couple measures from a hymn—and then listen for the echo that came back

amazingly clear, leaving her with wonder about the energy behind those sound waves.

Thunderstorms were breathtaking. Mountains to the north and west provided sound boards which made the awesome thunder reverberate until the ground shook like an earthquake. Lightning often turned pink, it was so vivid. The valleys between the mountains became effective venturi-like funnels, causing the wind to blow more fiercely. The tall pine trees twisted in the wind like dancing dervishes. With the thunder as the tympani in the orchestra of the wind, a thought would fly through Jana's mind:

Isn't this where music comes from? Perhaps it is man's paltry attempt to imitate what God does by reflecting on nature and thinking it into being?

Jana was grateful for her Indian heritage, slight as it was. Her great-grandmother was a Cherokee, enough of a connection to make her think a lot about the Indian mind and spirit. Native Americans, she felt, respond to music in nature and give homage to natural things. Although colonial Americans perpetuated the image of savage pagans, Jana thought the Indians often revealed a greater appreciation of God in nature than modern man typically does. They spoke, for instance of the wind singing. They understood the roar of a waterfall and the soft song of the rain. Many modern people tend to be so busy and so quarantined from the natural world that they rarely hear the wind, the thunder, or the other voices of nature that filled the Indians with awe.

These musings led Jana to recall the Bible story of Moses going up to the mountain to receive the Ten Commandments. His people, warned to stay off the mountain, nevertheless "saw the thunderings, and the lightnings, and the noise of the trumpet." How remarkable, Jana thought,

that a musical instrument, the trumpet, is spoken of in the same breath as God's lightning and thunder.

Living for five years on a lake in the Virginia mountains where she could absorb the beauty and rhythms of the natural world was a gift to Jana. It became clear to her that a composer like Beethoven, too, must have understood the power of nature or he could not have written a work like the *Pastoral Symphony.*

It was liberating to be free of the confines and competitions of the musical world itself and to be able to spend time reflecting on the possibilities of creation, music, energy, the voice and mind of God, and how they all connected. But there still remained no possibility for expression of that wonder.

Chapter 29

CANTUS FIRMUS III: THE THEMES RECUR

usic had regained its central place in Jana's life during her years at Smith Mountain Lake. She and Jack founded a community chorus of sixty voices. The Fourth of July performances that Jana produced and conducted became a "must attend" for people throughout the western Virginia area. The state park became the venue for an all-day celebration every year, with food, picnics, and a boat parade. During the day, "Betsy Ross" and "Thomas Jefferson" and "George Washington" would roam the grounds talking with the people and discussing Revolutionary politics and how to make good beeswax candles or how to sew a good flag. With scores of boats moored in the swimming area bay, running lights twinkling, and families sprawled on the sand and in the grass, the day would end with a patriotic concert and fireworks.

These good times continued until Jack decided that he wanted to retire to Florida to enjoy virtually uninterrupted flying conditions with one of his aeronautical buddies. Jana and Jack sold their log house and, once resettled

in Stuart on Florida's east coast, Jana became interim choral director at a local community college forty miles north in Fort Pierce. These were happy years, too.

Tony Allo, Jana's supervisor and immediate boss at the college was a fine Christian man about her age and he loved to talk. And talk they did. His laugh was infectious and his faith was awesome. Jana had found someone with whom she could share some of her deep thoughts.

"Tony, do you ever wonder where music really came from?"

While Tony was a fairly uncomplicated man who did not dig into philosophical matters routinely, he was surely and solidly motivated by his faith. He would answer something like:

"It obviously comes from God ultimately, because he created everything anyway. But I do think that it is not accidental that the Psalms and the other songs of the scriptures play such a cardinal role in our faith lives."

Tony and his wife, Terry, made Jana feel worthwhile and the latitude he gave her as a teacher was more than gratifying. But it did not fully satisfy that odd longing she had to express something that seemed inexpressible. There were so many strands and threads of thought and knowledge about so many different things—science, philosophy, art, music, math—all of them tantalizing and yet evasive. Everything seemed to have one core and yet Jana could not for the life of herself articulate that core, and when she tried to talk about it to her friends, they either changed the subject or just became openly uneasy. She really felt alone in her quest.

Chapter 29

Jana had always been intrigued by Robert Shaw's declaration that:

"...half-ideas are transient-shaped—
If only they would stand completely still
Until one found the words their size.
You inventory your entire stock—and turn to find
You have a cubed suit for a sphered thought."

One of Jana's half-ideas was her belief that the "music of the spheres" and the music that nature itself "sings" are *pure music.* Man-made compositions, even the most sublime or grandiose, would thus, almost by definition, be but feeble attempts to reflect the magnificent and perfect music of the Creator. Whenever she voiced this line of thought, she was met with skepticism; it seemed too far "out of the box." When she was an undergrad, Joe Flummerfelt warned her not to take such lofty ideas to her grad school thesis committee, and, of course, he had been exactly right. The thesis committee wanted no part of such a subject for her master's work.

Now that she was teaching on the college level, Jana had opportunity to talk to Tony—and her students—about her thoughts, but no one could seem to be able to fathom the real depths of her quest for truth. What did the phrase "worship the Lord in the beauty of holiness" really mean? Was it in any way connected to the beauty and truth of true music, and, if it were, what constituted that true music?

Looking to science for information and possible answers, Jana recalled that she was told in her youth that the atom was the smallest parti-

cle of matter. Then they split the atom. "Split the atom!" was what Shaw yelled at the choir when he was teaching his singers to evoke the pangs of death in Verdi's Requiem. Why did he use that metaphor? Jana's aleatory song continued to sing on in her heart, unabated and evasive.

All too soon Tony retired from the community college, the professor whom Jana had been replacing returned from his sabbatical, and life changed one more time. Jana resigned her position at the college.

Chapter 30

OFFERTORIUM

ozart's *Requiem* embodies the idea of offertory. The translation from the Latin contains the following phrases:

"Lord Jesus Christ, King of glory, liberate the souls of the faithful.

Let the standard-bearer, holy Michael, bring them into holy light,

which was promised to Abraham and his descendants.

Sacrifices and prayers of praise, Lord, we offer to You."

At this point in her life, Jana made a conscious decision to make an offering of her own. And it was not a sad time, necessarily. She longed to have her own thoughts to be liberated by finding her Holy Grail and finding the "holy light" that would make sense of the quest she had been on for most of

her life. Perhaps—perhaps—by giving her energies to the realization of Jack's dreams, she could find a new pathway to understanding. Love and living had to be closely related. Didn't God allow Himself to be called Love? Must love, then, not be bound up in beauty and music?

She had enjoyed five years of being immersed in music in Florida. Her work as choral director at the community college carried additional responsibilities as vocal coach for the drama department. She was teaching music theory and coaching a very fine string quartet. Tony even saw to it that she had opportunities to conduct his jazz ensemble. Not that she felt very safe in that role, but Tony was encouraging and the students did not laugh too hard at her awkward attempts to be "cool."

But now, Jack had received a call from one of his aviation contacts in Delaware—one of the DuPont family who owned an airport in a small town near Wilmington—asking him to come back north to start a flight school on their campus. Jack had been involved in running a flight school in Florida, and, in fact, had established a flight program between that school and the college where Jana had been teaching. At age 75, Jack was strong and virile and still very full of himself. He presented the idea to Jana. His logical mind made a persuasive case for the move:

"We are not getting any younger and while we still have the good health and the desire to move forward, I think we should do it. Besides, we old pilots are a dying breed and we should give our best to the kids while we still can. What do you say?"

What could she say? No? And remember, Jana had her own set of cavalier ambitions. She was very proud of being one of only three or four thousand female flight instructors in the country at that time—in the mid-to-late-90's—and her sense of drama and excitement over life was being appealed to. Jack knew that, somehow.

132

Chapter 30

Within a few weeks, they had packed up enough clothes to see them through a season change in the northland, contacted a real estate agent about the eventual sale of their house, packed up their two cats, and flew away to their little cottage on the Chesapeake Bay. It was early March.

Chapter 31

VARIATIONS ON A THEME: 1

At first, there seemed to be little, if any, connection between Jana's passion for music and her love of flying. But as time unfolded and her experience in the air with the students became her norm, she began to notice undeniable comparisons between the two. Pythagoras had proven beyond any question that the ratio between frequencies produced pitches which could be manipulated by changing the length of the strings being plucked. There was also a very constant ratio relationship between airspeed, lift, and the stalling point of a given airplane. Depending upon the design of the aircraft and its wing, this ratio remained inviolable. Slow down too much in the final turn before landing and the inevitable result would be a stall-spin accident. Fascinating!

To say nothing of rate of turn and angle of bank-speed ratios.

Then, there was that on-going little argument between Jana and Jack, which always made the instructors in their school chuckle. Jana declared that she could always tell when the engines of the airplanes were not running

well. She would come dashing up the steps at the school office, calling out to Jack at the top of her voice:

"I heard it again! We have to take 6393G over to the maintenance hangar and have Bill look at it before it completely quits. The timbre of the engine changes when you hit 1800 RPM and I can feel it shudder!"

Jack was not ever convinced. "There is nothing wrong with that engine. The mag check is perfect and we are not burning oil or using too much fuel!"

"I don't care about that. I can feel a harmonic change in the floor boards when it happens and I can hear something falter in the sound!"

This conversation always ended with the very same comment. Jack would grimace and moan, "Musicians! They are all alike and have big imaginations. Guys, there is nothing wrong with 6393G. It is just Jana's imagination."

And then came the cold January day when Jana had to ferry 6393G to another airport. Jack had driven her to Wilmington Airport and dropped her off to fly the airplane and had told her he would see her at the Summit Airport in an hour. He left. Jana's friend, Barbara, was on duty in the Wilmington Control Tower.

As Jana was taxiing out to the runway, the engine abruptly faltered and quit. Thinking she had simply throttled too quickly, Jana started the engine again and continued out for her take-off clearance. Barbara announced:

"O.K., 6393G cleared for take-off. Southwest bound, 1500 feet, left turn-out approved. Have a good one, Jana!"

"Thanks, Wilmington. See you tomor—! What the—Hey, Barb! My engine is wanting to quit! Hang on, maybe, Uh! Oh! It just quit!"

136

"Citation on down-wind for 1. Divert immediately. We have an engine failure in progress off of the end of 9." That was Barbara clearing the area for 6393G.

"O.K., Jana. Say your altitude."

"Five hundred feet." 6393G always climbed well, thank goodness! "Barb, I'm already turned in for Runway 1. I think I have plenty of altitude…"

"Cleared to land!" And then Barbara kept up a line of cheerful chatter about how well Jana had negotiated her left turn to Runway 1 behind the Citation, just to keep things from getting too dramatic.

Two hours later, Bill, the mechanic, delivered Jana to the Summit Airport where Jack was waiting with a somewhat chagrined look on his face. Jana had called him as soon as she could, but he had had a few moments of wondering where his wife was and under his chagrin, was genuinely glad to see her.

"I knew you could handle anything that came along, J. You did splendid!"

How did he know?

"The next time I tell you that there is a change in timbre in the engine, will you believe me and understand that it means things are not right? If it's supposed to run smooth at 1800, it will run smooth at 1800 unless there is something wrong!"

And there was good reason for the rough harmonic that Jana both felt and heard. A cylinder was, as Bill put it, "trying to stick." When it finally did, it simply quit. Hadn't Jana felt the same thing under her feet at the Duomo in Spoleto?

Chapter 32

VARIATIONS ON A THEME: 2

Then, there was the time that Jana and Jack were flying to Columbia, South Carolina to see Jana's daughter. The two cats, who, by the way, loved to fly, were safe in the back seat in their carriers. The day was grey, with low clouds that periodically dropped a curtain of rain from their laden folds and it was fun to watch that curtain form and then dissipate. It was intriguing, too, to fly through that curtain, although, sometimes, it could be very bumpy in there because of drastic temperature changes. Jack teased that the airplane needed washing anyway. But a very strange thing happened.

There was a particularly heavy curtain of rain up ahead. Jana complained about the bumps but Jack turned 6393G toward the rain and flew directly into it. As the fuselage became entirely engulfed in the rain, it suddenly began to hum. The whole aircraft began to hum! Jack's head whipped around toward Jana, his eyes wide.

"What is that?"

Jana could not even find her voice. As suddenly as they had flown into the rain, they flew out and the humming stopped. There was very little conversation now as the two tried to figure out what had happened. Ahead there was another curtain of rain, into which Jack promptly flew. And again, the humming returned, even louder this time. The rain was heavier. It was low-throated and sounded more like a soft pedal stop on an organ than anything else Jana could think of. Kind of there-but-not-there, like the "C" pedal point on the organ in the Charles Ives Psalm 90.

The only explanation Bill could give later on was that the radio antennae wire on the top of the airplane must have picked up a harmonic from the engine or the friction of the wet air against the airplane itself.

This experience only added to the conviction growing in Jana's mind that all things—even airplanes—have a musical component that no one had been able to explain up to this point.

140

Chapter 33

CANTUS FIRMUS: IV

The old themes kept replaying themselves. Jana could not stay away from her own thoughts and they kept reverting to that longing—that nagging conviction that there was so much more to the whole discipline of music than what was taught in music schools worldwide. Of course, this was a huge, larger-than-life idea that was forming in her mind, but Jana had always had to cope with a brain that worked overtime and that lived, for the most part, outside the box. She liked that term. It gave her permission to think the expansive thoughts that came so easily to her.

One thing was bothering her immensely at this stage. She and Jack had begun attending a large Methodist church near Wilmington, Delaware. The people were very caring and friendly, but the music was a total disaster in Jana's mind. She had been safely ensconced in the Episcopal church for several years and so had remained quite well inoculated against the vast changes that were taking place in the contemporary, evangelical churches. On Christmas Eve of 1997, she was stunned to hear a diminutive blonde drummer sing "O Holy Night" accompanied by the rock band that she was leading from the

drum set. That was the beginning of another rebirth of energetic drive in her quest for truth in music. She could never leave it alone for very long at a time.

She came home from the airport one day to find Jack wearing a broad grin. "I think that is something you would be interested in doing." He nodded toward a brochure on the kitchen counter.

"His manner was far different than Earle's, wasn't it?" Jana mused. *"Like he is really wanting me to get interested again in thinking, dreaming, writing, not telling me how to lead my life."*

The brochure was from Calvin College in Grand Rapids, and it described a symposium that would be held the end of January on theology and the arts—in the quest of a theology *of* the arts!

"EJ!" That was her pet name for Jack. "EJ! This is wonderful. Maybe they are having the same misgivings that I am! Can I go?"

Up to now, she didn't have any idea of the "culture" and "worship" wars that were raging all across the country.

At the symposium, Jana met the man who was chair of the worship department and head of the music department at Calvin. He was very interested in her embryonic ideas about the origins of music, the true meanings of music, and agreed to send her a copy of the manual that his team was developing as a guideline for a theology of the arts curriculum in the future. When it arrived at her home weeks later, Jana devoured all of the articles, took notes, and wrote volumes in the margins. Her mind was off and running again. She would return to this place at Calvin several times in the course of her impending journey of discovery.

Chapter 34

QUASI UNA FANTASIA E BRILLIANTE

ife can become very mundane. Even teaching flying
can take on a mantel of sameness—not really boredom—
but sameness.

"Keep on the center line."

"Watch your air speed."

"Drop the nose."

"Right rudder."

Every student eventually must learn the same lessons and the good instructor soon learns how to make those lessons most easily accessible. But
then something will suddenly flash onto the pallet of life in brilliant color and
change the entire landscape.

Jack had sent Jana to Wal-Mart to get some office supplies. Ever since
her trip to Calvin College, Jana had been grappling with a new resolve to start
writing down the thoughts that had been growing in her mind for so many

years. The only problem was that these thoughts were burgeoning and terribly mercurial. Jana kept remembering Robert Shaw's poem about the "cubed suit for the sphered thought." That described her vagrant mental wanderings so well. But she had to start somewhere, didn't she? And her magnetic memory still worked so well, too. She could even recall what she was wearing when she ran into the Wal-Mart on that hot summer day. Her maroon flight suit was sticking to her back with perspiration.

She headed for the stationery department and quickly grabbed two spiral notebooks, one small to carry with her all the time, and a large one to keep at home for serious journaling. As she turned to find the paper clips, she heard a quiet voice with a distinct Southern accent say, "You findin' everything you lookin' for, ma'am?"

Standing at the end of the kiosk was a rather small-statured black woman with closely cropped, very silky, curly hair. There was a large space between her teeth and her smile was almost as engaging as Walt Rybeck's smile had been so long ago.

Jana thought, *"If this woman were white she could be Walt's sister."* Odd. "Yes, I just picked up some notebooks and I'm looking for the paper clips."

The woman's sparkling black eyes smiled, too, and what happened next was astounding. She began to speak to Jana in that quiet voice, but now in a vernacular that sounded almost prophetic, and she did not give Jana a chance to respond.

"You're goin' to write a book, aren't you? That's a good thing. But remember, you must set your face like a flint, and don't be afraid of their faces. You must not be ashamed to say what you believe and don't let anything stop you. You will be guided as you go…"

Chapter 34

There was more, but it was the sudden impact of this woman's complete understanding of what Jana was thinking that astounded her. She asked the woman her name.

"My name is Jacquie."

"Will I see you again?"

"I don't know. That is up to the Lord."

And she turned quietly and walked away. When Jana returned to the Wal-Mart several days later to look for "Jacquie," no one knew who she was, and she never saw her again.

Jana made an entry in her journal on July 28, 2000: "I met an angel in Wal-Mart today and I believe she spoke prophecy to me."

Chapter 35

ATTACA

*T*he summer of 2000 was to be a pivotal time in Jana's and Jack's lives, but they would not realize that for another year. They signed a contract to teach young men from the United Arab Emirates how to fly, with the caveat that they did not have to know how to land or take off. Only to handle the airplane in the air and follow visual clues like roads or rivers. Their native Air Force would teach them everything else. Little did they know that their flight school had been targeted along with many others to train men for the impending terrorist attack the following year.

Of course, by the early autumn of 2001, life had changed for everyone, and most of all for people like Jana and Jack. The fall of the twin towers took away the carefree joy of being in the air, dancing among the clouds and seeing young fledgling pilots earn their wings. In addition, the sudden realization that your organization had been part of the diabolical plot was a sickening realization.

The FAA and the FBI had actually been very understanding in their investigations of JHarris Aviation's student records; they questioned every

147

phase of the summer of 2000, trying to connect the dots between irrelevancy and relevancy. Whoever would have known that America could be struck like this? By Christmas of 2001, Jana and Jack had sold their business, their home in Delaware, and had bought a new home in Pompano Beach, Florida.

Jack had become very interested in the ministry of Dr. D. James Kennedy at Coral Ridge Presbyterian in Fort Lauderdale. He and Jana joined the choir there and Jana took over one of the children's choirs. New friends, new challenges, new way of life—again. But it was short-lived.

By the late summer of 2003, Jana was beginning to really chafe at the bit—she needed to get on with her writing and found herself to be very restless. A chain of odd events made it clear that Florida was not to be the final retirement location for Jana and Jack, and with the help of old friends, Harvey and Esther Olin of Smith Mountain Lake days, they relocated to Forest, Virginia, near Lynchburg and Liberty University.

Part 3
RECAPITULATION

Chapter 36

MUSICA ATTACA

usic is a moral law.

It gives a Soul to the universe,

Wings to the mind,

Flight to the imagination,

A Charm to sadness, and Life to everything.—Plato

These words from the pen of the great philosopher, Plato, took on sudden significance for Jana: *music and flight!* Music gives a soul to the universe and flight to the mind and imagination. Her two great loves! Music and flight! But those last words: Life to *everything*!

Moving back to the mountains proved to be a tonic for Jana for a while. Jack's and Jana's new home was within sight of the Blue Ridge foothills which really did reflect a hint of bluish haze, especially in the heat of late summer afternoons. 2003 and 2004 had evaporated into that haze, it seemed,

and still there was no real breakthrough in her writing or sense of direction about what to do next. But her mind continued to work overtime on all the "transient half-ideas" that were congregating there unbidden and from many unrelated sources. Not the least of which was the keen mind of Jana's friend, Esther Olin. They had been friends since the Smith Mountain Lake days.

Jana recalled Jack's impression of Esther when they met her for the first time at New London Airport years before. She had agreed to meet to discuss whether or not she would accept Jana's invitation to become the accompanist for the newly founded Smith Mountain Arts Council Chorale—nicknamed the SMAC Chorale. They had just flown over to Forest from Smith Mountain and were standing under the wings of the airplane. Esther was perusing the Bach Cantata that Jana had chosen:

"I've never played this particular cantata, but it does not look too daunting. What tempo have you set for this opening?"

She pointed to the orchestral parts on the opening page. Even Esther's mode of dress implied a no-nonsense woman of strong character and opinionated bearing—in the best sense of the words. It was obvious that she was familiar with doing things in a finely honed and well-organized way. The only problem was that Jana, having sung *Christ Lag in Todesbanden* several times with the Westminster Choir, had not yet bothered to analyze her own approach to the music. As a conductor, she was still behind the "power curve." Her reply was, as a result, and to say the least, halting.

"Uh, well, uh, hmmmm. I've sung this work many times, but, umm, I just received the music yesterday and I haven't…"

Esther was still undaunted, laughed the raucous laugh that Jana would come to adore hearing, and said, "Good. I'll do it! See you Monday night at the Methodist Church!'"

Jack's blue eyes twinkled as Esther turned and walked away. "Well, Jana, I think you have just met your 'come-uppance!'"

Esther seemed to revel in presenting Jana with questions that might trip her up—or at least, make her think more seriously about her theories:

"If all music is an attempt to reflect God-given beauty, how does a genre like acid rock fit in? Or the drug culture that avidly pursues the rock culture? Or the poignant drone of a bagpipe? Or the music used to promote sales in the malls? Do these have any relation to the sounds of radio waves from the stars or the whistles and slides that accompany the aurora borealis that you keep talking about?"

Jana could count on Esther for a challenge. If the answer didn't satisfy Esther's sense of logic, she would toss her head back, laugh that wondrous, raucous laugh and say, "That's hysterical!"

Esther was highly intelligent and pragmatic, a woman who had come through more than her share of troublesome things in life with a strong grip on reality and faith. And she proved to be a wonderful sounding board for the tumbling ideas and theories that bounded through Jana's mind during this very formative period of learning and thinking.

Jana was a born teacher. She recalled her very first piano student, a young soldier at West Point who was from California. He said his thirteen year old teacher was the best friend he had during those awful years when he was serving his country so far from home. He was probably eight or nine years older that Jana, but the music made them friends.

Over the ensuing years, Jana had the privilege of working with and encouraging many fine students but none surpassed Connor. Jana first met Connor when he was five and was a member of her children's choir

at church. It was obvious immediately that this child was gifted with more than intelligence.

Connor had dark hair and big soulful dark brown eyes. Elusive dimples showed only when he smiled broadly or was thinking deep thoughts—which he frequently did. He had showed that spark of deep understanding of the things of beauty even as a five year old. He loved the younger kids in the choir and was always trying to help them. Susan, Connor's mother, cautioned Jana that he might be a handful, and if he were, she would not be upset if Jana had to drop him from the choir. Such was not the case; Jana simply made Connor the keeper of the "little ones" and he turned out to be the epitome of kindness and help as the choir monitor.

Between that time and the time that Jana became Connor's piano teacher, his parents bought him an electronic keyboard, albeit a good one. The Clavinova was expensive, but it was still an electronic instrument and did not embody the characteristics of an organic instrument. When Connor sat for the first time at Jana's "huge" Baldwin grand piano, he instantaneously fell out of love with his Clavinova. He called it an "unnatural instrument." That began his very pointed and personal campaign for a grand piano of his own.

His intellect did not stop at the artistic. He loved sleight of hand and did it well. He also designed, built, and flew all manner of paper airplanes and delighted in flying them from the upstairs landing.

At his lesson on a particular day, Connor complained that he had not slept well the night before.

"But that doesn't matter. I just lay in bed and told myself riddles and I have a good one for you, Ms. Jana. 'What do you call a rock keyboard player who sells his Klavinova and buys a grand piano and learns to play Beethoven's Fur Elise on it?'"

Jana feigned ignorance and confusion.

"I have no idea! What would you call him?"

Connor assumed a wise look.

"Cured!"

His pianistic and musical skills grew rapidly. It was obvious, though, that his innate talent and his incredible ear for music surpassed his physical strength and challenged Jana to know how to handle his development. After one year of study, Connor was asked to play in a recital at another teacher's studio. The cross between elation and fright that exhibited itself in the youngster made Jana smile as she remembered her own early ascent into the world of accomplished musicians at such an early age.

But Connor also gave Jana courage. Here was a child with an inherent understanding of some of the deepest of musical truths. Oh, that she should lead him well.

Over the ensuing year, Connor continued to mature as a pianist and as a talented youngster. As he approached his eleventh birthday, he was preparing to play the entire Beethoven Fur Elise in recital, from memory, of course. More than that, he had begun to develop a keen appreciation for his talent and the responsibility of living up to it. Perhaps he would accept the mantel of artistic integrity when Jana was ready to pass it on.

Chapter 37

MYSTERIOSO: FINDING MEANING

There were several intertwined ideas that had launched Jana's quest for truth and it was difficult for her to articulate them, even to herself. She started out by musing over the origins of music and what its real power could be. This notion encompassed the whole immense concept of the singing cultures of the world and why they sang. Especially the Hebrew nation. Their entire life was a matter of song: worship, birth, death, battle, fear, triumph, and yet there was a certain mystery surrounding their music—there simply was not much information about it historically. The mystery was compounded by the understanding that their spiritual culture was, in all likelihood, musical throughout.

Then there was the whole mystery of beauty. Jana had met a young man at one of the worship and the arts conferences she attended. He had written his PhD dissertation on "beauty." A question kept replaying itself in Jana's brain: *"What is the 'beauty of holiness?' And does it have any musical connotation?"*

What about the mystery of matter and creation? Jana recalled learning about the atom at the end of World War II—*the atom was the smallest particle of matter*—but then, they split the atom! "Split the atom!" was what Shaw had yelled at the choir when teaching his singers to evoke the pangs of death in Verdi's Requiem.

There were other mysteries that occupied Jana's mind along with a growing awareness that everything in creation was, as Einstein had suggested in his quest for the "theory of everything," related and probably governed by the same set of simple natural laws. A recurring theme: a cantus firmus.

The mystery of healing. A new idea of modern medicine, based on psychological experiments, suggested that music has healing power and can be an antidote for depression, insomnia, and the pain of labor. New and modern? In ancient days, as the Old Testament says, "when the evil spirit was upon Saul," David played his harp and "Saul was refreshed and was well, and the evil spirit departed from him." And then, Jana's memory would revert immediately to that tiny blue and creamy-yellow sick room of long ago and that beautiful music that had kept the little girl from succumbing to the illness that gripped her.

The mystery of mathematical structure. The bonds between math and music, described so well by Edward Rothstein, New York Times journalist, peaked Jana's curiosity when she considered that, perhaps, the music and poetry she loved was so satisfying because of its mathematical order. What did it say about Twentieth century culture, she wondered, that so much of modern verse and music was designed to shatter any sense of regularity? Were so many poets and composers out of touch with the order that keeps the universe in its orbits? Was that a deliberate attack against God's order of things?

158

Rothstein's writings gave Jana more than a little encouragement. He explained Galileo's theory that certain numerical relations made "some combinations of tones more pleasing than others," and of Euclid's similar mathematical analysis of music some 2,000 years earlier. Pythagoras shared this idea and based on its merit, he crafted the basis of both mathematics and today's western musical harmonic structure. An 18th century mathematician, Leonard Euler, wrote a discourse on the relationship of consonance to whole numbers. The great astronomer Kepler believed the planets' revolutions literally created a "music of the spheres," a sonic counterpart to the mathematical laws of planetary motion that he unraveled.

The mystery of the universe. Albert Einstein's Holy Grail was to find a "means of describing nature's forces within a single, all-encompassing, coherent framework. His was a passionate belief that the deepest understanding of the universe would reveal its truest wonder: the simplicity and power of the principles on which it is based."[iii] Einstein's earliest impetus was to find the "theory of everything": one single, simple, and beautiful set of laws that would perfectly organize and describe all of the universe and its workings. His entire theory of relativity was formulated as a result of this quest.

The mystery of cohesion. The more Jana investigated the many mysteries of many disciplines, the more it struck her that, beneath the myriad variations and differentiations that confront us, was a cohesiveness suggesting a surprising degree of unity and interconnectivity. This reinforced her determination to devote all her energies to pursue the

---

[iii] *The Elegant Universe:* Brian Greene: W. W. Norton & Company, Inc. 1999

questions that finally, after more than twenty years of pondering, were beginning to take some vague shape.

The mystery of music itself. Jana had discovered a book by a British scholar by the name of Jeremy Begbie[iv] several years before moving to Lynchburg. In the Introduction to his work, Begbie made a cryptic statement which became the articulation of the question which had been lurking in Jana's mind for years:

"It is clear *that* music is one of the most powerful communicative media we have, but *how* it communicates and *what* it communicates are anything but clear."

If she could just find a satisfactory answer to this query, it would solve everything, she mused.

In fact, a metamorphosis in Jana's thinking struck her as quite remarkable: Although she was still deeply curious about the origins of music and its ultimate place in the total scheme of things, she sensed a dawning realization that her quest necessarily focused not only on the origin of music but on the origin of all things. And more important than that, if she could only find that one linking pin which would explain how the origins of music and creation were related, the answer to both queries would be complete. We would be able to understand Einstein's quest and would be able to see how all things are related and held together.

It seemed a short leap from the beauty around her to the belief that one loving God—not chance or random accidents—was responsible for all this beauty and harmony. Many of her colleagues, coming from different religious backgrounds than Jana, found this hard to accept, but she

---

[iv]   Begbie, Jeremie S., *Theology, Music and Time*, Cambridge University Press, 2000

was long accustomed to standing alone in her convictions. Yet an innocent question from her husband threw her a curve:

"So God created all things," Jack said. "But where did He get the raw materials? The laws of nature require a medium for construction and it seems unlikely God would violate His own laws to accomplish Creation."

Jana should not have been surprised by Jack's straightforward look at creation. After all, he was an engineer. Manufacturing was his milieu and he operated on the premises of structural law. Though she had taken the act of creation for granted, she had to admit Jack's question was reasonable and needed to be pursued.

Gradually, not like a bolt of lightning, the thought came to Jana that maybe God sang creation into existence. Perhaps, she was beginning to think, God was a singer.

Chapter 38

VOCA ME CUM BENEDICTUS: COUNT ME AS BLESSED

uring this phase of the development of her theories, Jana had an exciting experience. It came at a time when she especially needed encouragement to pursue her quest with intensity and not to become dejected from the fact that she stood so alone in that quest. After a long day of writing and seemingly getting nowhere, she went to Barnes and Noble, bought a couple of books and a CD of a Brahms violin piece and returned home to her writing. It often inspired her to have a favorite composer's work in the background while she worked.

Jana was only half listening when suddenly the atmosphere in the room became electrified and that familiar chilling sensation ran through her body. What was she hearing? Could it be? After sixty-five years of never knowing, could it be? It was! It was the sound that she longed for day after day in the little butter yellow and blue room back in Highland Falls, the mystery music she stayed alive to hear when the ravages of scarlet fever were threatening to take her life away.

She fairly flew to the CD player. Picking up the CD jacket, she read the inscription: Violin Sonata No. 3 in D minor, op. 108. This was the second movement. She heard the rising motif in the violin, still so familiar to her, the bursting beauty of an ascent completed in such abject peacefulness that it made her feel as if heaven itself had been attained at last.

Jana was running up two flights of stairs to EJ's sitting room, yelling, "I have found it! I have found it at last! You have to come and hear this!"

Her ebullience was almost frightening until EJ realized the import of Jana's discovery. He was overjoyed that after a lifetime she had retrieved this composition which finally had a name and a reality as well as a cherished memory. This great piece of music, penned by one of the monumental composers of the nineteenth century, took on an extra meaning for Jana now because Brahms was known as a man who, like her, feared God and recognized Him as the giver of musical creation. Much of Brahm's music struck many as beyond the bounds of the temporal.

As a pianist, Jana understood the eternality of Brahm's music. So often, the melodic and rhythmic structures were superimposed in such a way that there seemed to be no beginning and no end. The memories of the little blue and yellow bedroom flooded back into her consciousness. The fetid heat of the summer afternoon and the faint smell of illness were still burned into her brain. She could feel the eternal pull of the rising motif in the violin as if it were happening for the first time. The years vanished and Jana experienced the very first moment again. There was life in the sound, and she felt its power once more.

Chapter 39

*J*ana was exhilarated by her sense that perhaps music comprised God's creation tools, as it were, but she could not leave it at that. She realized that what resonated within her would appear to others not only as unconventional but possibly outlandish—because it was so much beyond what they have been led to think. So she felt a need to find evidence or proof. Because her friend Esther was a composer, Jana told her she needed to know more about the creative process, how music is put together.

"Good grief," Esther laughed, "you've been a musician all your life and know enough about music. What you need to do is study Hebrew."

"Hebrew! Why in the world?"

Esther made a convincing case that, since Jana sincerely believed God sang the commands, she should go to the root source, the language of her Bible. It was an epiphany. No need for further discussion. Within a couple of weeks Jana had enrolled at Liberty University in Lynchburg and had be-

gun auditing a course in Hebrew translation tools by Dr. Ronald Giese. She started learning the alphabet, vocabulary, and elementary grammar. She and Ron almost spontaneously became friends.

One day after class, Dr. Giese called Jana aside and gave her a couple of his Hebrew poetry and literature books along with a small manual explaining the intricacies of Hebrew poetic techniques like parallelism. She became intrigued by the account of God's conversation with Job and the inferences that there was some unrevealed force with which God was very familiar but which hid itself from Job completely. "To what were the foundations (of the earth) fastened?—when the morning stars sang together and all the sons of God *shouted* for joy?"

Jana ruminated over the myriads of experiences from her past where she had come face to face with the deep intuition that all of nature, being created by God Himself, was part of a glorious song. The sunset, the bird-song, the wind, the dark hues of late evening on the mountains, the aurora. But something else caught her attention, too. None of this beauty was happenstance. There was always incredible cohesion to everything and an irrefutable rhythm to things. It was as if all of the universe was singing one glorious song. Even the roses had a most remarkable pattern to their flowering buds and seemed to silently sing their own song.

Ever since undergraduate school, Jana had been mulling over the idea that, in the hierarchical scheme of things, speech was at the low end of the totem pole of vocal communication and took the least amount of energy to produce. The art of singing, on the other hand, commanded an energetic output that far exceeded that of speech. And the sounds created were diametrically different. The melodic character of sung sound had a beauty that even the most mellifluous speaking voice could not approach. In her most sanctified imagination, Jana could not envision the Almighty

166

Chapter 39

God standing, benignly, looking out over His vast, formless void, and simply saying:

"—and let there be—"

There had to be more drama, more effort, more energy than that. What if He took in an eternal, life-sustaining breath and sang:

"—and let there be—"

Jana's quest pursued her relentlessly.

Chapter 40

STRETTO: SAME THEME BUT DIFFERENT VOICE

ut it was not only her quest for answers to her questions of faith and religious compatibility that pursued her. She intuited that some of the greatest proofs of the unity of God's source as the Creator lay in the world of science. She could not rid herself of the idea that only a great Designer could have designed, created, and set in motion such magnificent evidences of His power.

Jana was not particularly well read in the sciences or mathematics, mostly because she simply had never been particularly interested in them. That is, she wasn't interested until she began to understand the deeper relationships between music and other disciplines—especially math and earth sciences. Her interest in physics was the slowest to find its place in the pattern of cohesion.

The best she could recall about physics was an awkward moment during her senior year when her model of the lift pump succeeded only in spraying red-colored water all over the high school principal one day while he was

standing in for the physics teacher in Fairmont, during that wonderful year when Walt was the center of her world. And all of that seemed to have no relevance at all in her musings over the cohesiveness of all creation.

Somewhere along the way, Jana recalled the article written by Edward Rothstein entitled, "Math and Music: The Deeper Links." The article sub-title had read: "How Two Abstract Systems Reshape Our Understanding of Reality." It appeared that there were many highly intellectual people out there who were chasing the same vague idea that there was a magnificent interconnection that provided some reasonable logic to trying to solve the dilemma: how do things relate or do they? Apparently they do relate, or else people like Edward Rothstein would not take the time nor spend the energy to "relate" music to math and try to develop the relationship between the two and even go so far as to say that these two very diametrically opposed disciplines give us "reshaped" understanding of our reality as creatures of the universe.

True, Rothstein was making the comparison between mathematics and music, but by this time Jana was almost convinced that music had eternal and irrefutable religious, if not completely Divine, beginnings. And maybe there was no beginning. Maybe music was part of the first causes—*the primum movens*.

That gave real credibility to Rothstein in Jana's mind. She felt that the underlying strength of reason could be found in the earliest writings of men such as Plato, Aristotle, and Pythagoras. Jana reflected that perhaps the Greeks had a much keener understanding of the relationships and connections among disciplines than modern man has. She recalled one of her professors at Westminster lecturing once on the Doctrine of the Ethos of Music. The early Greek philosophers seemed to see quite clearly the necessity for order, equilibrium, and harmony for the survival of the human organism. These values were seen as one of the most elevated planes of the spiritual life: music. And the Greeks could see the moral force exerted by music in the education of the mind, soul, and behavioral patterns of humankind. It was an important message that crossed centuries of the accrual of knowledge.

Off and on over the next twenty years or so, the Pythagorean theorem, the Golden Rectangle, and the Golden Mean would surface and Jana would dig out that article and read it again. She grappled with its ramifications, but never seemed to have enough peace and quietude in her life to just sit down and hammer it through so that she could understand it.

As time progressed she became more curious about the connections between music, math, and other sciences like astronomy. Or engineering and aeronautics. Or biology and genetics. She heard that even our human DNA has a musical component and that frequencies can be assigned to differing DNA strands.

It seemed that the further Jana went along her route of discovery and the more she learned, the more questions surfaced to tantalize her. But in her mind, the gap between science and theology and the arts was narrowing exponentially. She was convinced in her sanctified imagination, but she knew that intuition and imagination were not enough to provide credibility for a theory.

Nonetheless, the laws of counterpoint demanded resolution and Jana felt assured that they would hold true. In time.

Chapter 41

EPISODE: MORE QUESTIONS AND MORE CONNECTIONS

The contrapuntal nature of Jana's discoveries about theology and science were astounding. All of academia seemed agreed in the twentieth century that there was little, if any, point of contact between theology and science. But the study of Hebrew opened up a commanding new understanding of the vibrancy of theological truth. It was no longer just a system of beliefs punctuated by rules and regulations governing every possible facet of life. It had become a vital and living way of life that had breath and a strong pulse which shaped it into a living thing. The Hebrew language lent an intuitive undergirding to that idea of theology as a living thing. And there was a rhythm to the language and rhythm to the life that it imparted. The astounding realization was that it *was actually music* that lay at the bedrock of that new concept.

The scriptures were alive with musical references. The Psalms ceased to be simply beautiful poetry which spoke of the existence of Yahweh and the singing of praises to Him. They became songs of ultimate beauty and holiness and the words of the original language were rich with melody and

harmony and the rhythm of the life that was in them. And it seemed that the God of Israel reveled in the singing of His children. Jana mused over what the melodies of those Psalms must have been like, accompanied by "timbrals and harps." It must have been glorious.

Isaiah 44:23 (NIV) took on new life as well in the light of Jana's new thinking:

> *"Sing for joy, O heavens, for the Lord has done this; shout aloud, O earth beneath. Burst into song, you mountains, you forests and all your trees, for the Lord has redeemed Jacob, he displays his glory in Israel."*

Music everywhere! The heavens were told to "sing for joy"; the earth was told to burst into song along with the mountains and forests and all of the trees! What a glorious sound that must be, Jana thought. And she was convinced that it was not a figure of speech. She knew in her spirit that when the scriptures said that the mountains burst into song, there was truth—the mountains *did sing*—and how she wished she could hear their song.

It occurred to Jana that the Scriptures were also replete with references to the scientific world. But it did seem that these references were far more veiled and difficult to uncover than those dedicated to the music of praise, for instance.

A favorite story from the Old Testament suddenly made exciting sense to Jana. When she was a young girl, the story of the walls of Jericho falling down in a tumble when the priests blew the trumpets and shouted always piqued her curiosity. How could that happen? But now

she could imagine that it was entirely feasible. Harmonics! Of course! If all of the universe is held together with strands of vibrating energy, then any interruption of that energy would cause a crash. Galloping Gertie; the floor of the Duomo in Spoleto; the walls of Jericho.

And the marvelous counterpoint of faith and science began to take on new life. Here was the convergence. Here was the point at which the two themes began to meld. There really was no vast distance between the theological and the scientific. The metaphors of the scriptures were actually scientific in their expressivity: the natural world is musical. The metaphors of scientific explanation were actually musical in their expressivity: perhaps the scientific world is more easily understood in musical terms. It seemed an easy leap for Jana to intuit that all of what we know of science dances with musical vibrancy.

Jana was beginning to see reason for the depths of experience she had been exposed to over a long lifetime. God wastes nothing, she thought. She began to take stock of her lifelong journey of discovery filled with music, echoing in her very soul and reflecting a wonder that Jana felt emanated from God Himself.

It had indeed been a long journey.

Chapter 42

TRANSITION

*J*ana enjoyed engaging her friend, Esther on the subject of God as the Master Musician. She enjoyed discussing the creative act as a musical event which might have used musical building blocks as the raw materials out of which the universes and galaxies and all that was in them were made. Esther was never quite fully committed to the idea. Intrigued but not committed—or at least, that is the position she conveyed.

"It is true, Jana, that it seems no one has ever specifically and dogmatically written anything about the possibility that God sang the Creation commands. However, legend carries snippets of information about the genesis of things being in song. And then, there is the Silmarillion of Tolkien and C. S. Lewis's Narnia. Hmmm…"

Jana's son, Kenneth, had brought these two works to her attention several years prior. Now, at Esther's behest, Jana pulled the volumes off the shelf again and started to read each in its turn with more seriousness. She was, to say the least, astounded at the similarities to her own thinking.

God's Song

C. S. Lewis had always been one of Jana's favorite authors, probably because he wrote from the point of view that all things originate with God and that all imaginative inventions must reflect God's truth. But Jana had never read the *Chronicles of Narnia* before, and so it was exciting for her to discover that in *The Magician's Nephew*, the great lion, Aslan, actually sang Narnia into existence. And the symbolism of the Lion as the Singing Creator also intrigued Jana. She seemed to recall hearing one of her Sunday School teachers referring to Jesus Christ as the all-powerful and majestic "Lion of God."

The writings of J. R. R. Tolkien were less familiar to Jana, but the discovery of *The Silmarillion* only served to stir her interest in Lewis' conviction that imaginative inventions were worthless unless they conveyed Truth. This idea seemed to be evident in Tolkien's portrayal of the creator god, Iluvatar, who brought the Ainur into being by his thought and then gave them a mighty theme with which they were to make a "Great Music" with harps and lutes and pipes and trumpets and with singing choirs. The very beauty of this Music was to go out into the void and by its power the void would become complete and no longer void, but pleasing and beautiful.

Jana was stunned to discover a bit later in the narrative that the creature Melkor became proud and convinced that his music should become better than that of his brethren. His prideful thoughts were woven into his singing and by them discord rose up and the beauty of the melodies of Iluvatar's musicians foundered in a sea of turbulent sound.

Jana read until she was convinced that the insights written here were really fashioned to portray truth in a fantastically literary way. She wondered, *"Maybe this is not really allegory. Could it be, like Lewis says, 'an imaginative invention?' Could this story hold the seeds of truth that describe music as the source of creation, ruined by the prideful singing that ruined the heavenly musician, Heylel, Lucifer, Satan?"*

Indeed, Jana's imagination was challenged yet one more time. She began to search around for more inferences that music was the stuff of creation—it just could be. But again, her thinking was capricious and fantasy-like, not concentrated and organized. Her curiosity was consuming and she spent hours surfing the internet for added information. And then she found this: the Apache Creation Story.

> *"In the beginning nothing existed—no earth, no sun, no moon, only darkness was everywhere. Suddenly from the darkness emerged a small bearded man, Creator, the One Who lives above. 'Where is the earth? Where is the sky?' he asked, and then sang, 'I am thinking, thinking, thinking what I shall create. Let us make earth. I am thinking of the earth, earth, earth; I am thinking of the earth,' he sang. The Creator sang, 'World is now made.' Then he began a song about the sky. He sang about it four times and made a sky."*[v]

The same story told of a great flood. The mention of the flood in this same Apache narrative added credibility to the idea that this allegorical story from Indian lore must have, as C. S. Lewis would say, origins of God's truth, since everything came from God in the first place.

As Jana continued to search for anecdotes and stories, she unearthed legend after legend in folklore from virtually every continent describing

[v] http://www.ilhawaii.net/~stony/lore34.html

creator gods who sang their various creations into being. It was extraordinary; this thread that wove through pagan literature as well as Christian—this thread weaving accounts of the singing creator.

It seemed that Jana had a gift for relating remote ideas and using them to reinforce each other. These writings all had a common theme, just like a chaconne or passacaglia. The embellishments and variations could be myriad, but they were all bound together by a common harmonic or rhythmic motif.

This half-idea could become pivotal.

Chapter 43

THEME II: RELIGION, FAITH, AND THE HEBREW LANGUAGE

ventually, Jana was able to begin the arduous work of putting random notes and thoughts into order. It was a difficult task to give the strength of her convictions to the words on the paper. Months went by and the work progressed very slowly. Life and family had to go on, but her mind persistently went back to her very early childhood, that little blue and cream yellow room and that beautiful music. Being snatched from the talons of death itself by the unutterable beauty and order of the second Brahms' violin sonata was a memory that held Jana transfixed for virtually all of her life. She could never escape the power of that experience.

Dr. Flummerfelt was right. The liberal university had no tolerance for the idea of God and certainly not for a God Who made music. But Jana had kept her original document framing the seminal ideas of her thesis and found great solace in the fact that what she had written there over thirty years ago was exactly the embryonic form of the ideas that were growing in her mind and spirit now. She began to read from it:

181

"Curt Sachs, the great German musicologist, said, 'However far back we trace mankind, we fail to see the springing up of music.'"

"A painted relief, the Blind Harpist (was) found in a tomb in Memphis, Egypt, dated 1375-1360 B.C."

"A piece of pottery called the 'Attic Cup' (painted by) Brygos captured the intense emotions wrought by the impact of music, dated from the 5th century, B.C."

"II Chronicles 6: the Jewish worship system had evolved the professional musician who was responsible for all music used in worship."

"Plato: 'Music is highly important…its lofty purpose is to serve, to help in building up a harmonious personality and in calming the human passions.'"

"In the Jew we find an entirely different concept. And here is the crux of my entire theory on the origins of music. Music was, in fact, an organic part of the daily life of the Jew even before he was identified as a Jew. Every human concern from birth to death was linked to musical expression."

182

Chapter 43

"It is interesting to observe here that 'in the surprisingly large vocabulary of Hebrew music, the terms for vocal music outnumber by far the purely instrumental ones. The inference may be that the human spirit best expresses itself through its own medium, the human voice…'"

"'Many early Church Fathers felt, as did many Jews, that God could be worshipped only through the human voice.'"

It began to dawn on Jana that the genesis of her own thoughts was probably fixed in her young mind during that near-death experience when she was ten and that the strong faith of her parents, especially her father, had already set her course long before that. Her mother's love for flowers and birds and trees and her father's undeniable love for nature and the woods and lakes were as familiar to her as rain, sunshine, and starlight. And her dad always hummed or sang and her mom whistled. Primitive as it was, there was always music about in her home. They were simple, uninitiated folk, but the music was there, and it was somehow connected to their faith, as well. She began to put the pieces together.

Something else had been commanding Jana's curiosity for many years. She cherished literature and words and poetry and the Bible. She was particularly fond of the Psalms in the Old Testament. Being a musician, she was intrigued by the constant reference to the "Chief Musician" and the basic theme of music coursing throughout that particular book of the Bible. But no one was ever able to tell her the real reason for the inclusion of that book in the canon of scripture, and as a child, when she

discovered that the Psalms were also part of the Hebrew writings from antiquity, she had a deep intuitive feeling that there was a good reason for that—but what was it? Yes, we were taught to praise God and sing His praise. Any good Catholic or Protestant knew that. But that did not tell anyone *why we were to sing* those praises. Much later, when she was studying with Paul Schocker, she came into contact with new knowledge: the Torah was sung by the Jewish cantor at services. She immediately asked *why?* Why not just read it?

There must be answers.

As life went on and education burgeoned, Jana continued growing in her conviction that there was some marvelous cohesiveness to all creation. The cosmos did not falter in its paths, art and literature had threads of commonality, mathematics and science vied for answers that would transcend their own formulae and equations and find resolution, and philosophy and religion argued over issues of eternal weight with no cohesive answers to man's quest for truth. The questions were always there. The answers were not. What had been so simple to believe when you were ten became insurmountable dilemmas when you were twenty. Challenge was on every hand, if one thought at all. But one thing over-rode all of the challenges and dilemmas—the centrality of God, Elohim. This, Jana felt deep in her soul.

All of these vagrant thoughts had common motifs: the origins of music, the inherent, irrevocable need for music throughout history and especially the history of the Hebrews, the evasive but burgeoning idea that vocal communication has a dedicated and maybe even holy posi-tion in the worship life of the human race. It was a growing mountain of evidential information. She shared these thoughts with her Hebrew class

Chapter 43

friend, Claude. Being an attorney he had a great grip on the logistics of argument and he helped Jana to think in a more convincingly logical way.

"You have an incredible imagination, Jana, and you must continue to give it to the Lord to use as you forge through these ideas. They are rather cutting edge, you know."

Another transient half-idea that had no roots yet and had no directive for being—just a thought—was: Creating anything is incredibly consuming in its necessity for discipline and devotion to its outcome. However, Jana was beginning to see God's creative energy somewhat differently as the magnificent, all-encompassing effort that hurled the galaxies into space and imbued them with the sustaining power that still maintains them in their orbits and in their flights to spaces unknown to man. She was beginning to intuit that energy as being musical in nature.

What if God *did* sing the commands at the moment of that initial burst of creative energy? She reflected on thoughts she had had a few years prior. She revisited some of her earlier writings:

> *"And so, 'in the beginning God' can take on new excitement. The simple language that was, and is, being used to relate or portray the Creation of the Universe in our Western educational world, leaves the scene open to all kinds of manipulation and even scornful explanation. As children in Sunday school, we heard that when 'God said' it happened and the imaginative world of the eager child in us was squashed into thinking that the event was not that monumental or else it would have made a bigger impression on our teachers."*

It was becoming more and more urgent to get to the end of the re-search and get these half-ideas forged into a cohesive theory which could be examined and analyzed, for better or for worse.

She turned to the Scriptures themselves, in view of the fact that the church of the twenty-first century seemed to be on a slippery slope theologically. She found no support there for her ideas; the church had enough struggles of its own and the average clergyman was reluctant to get entwined in this kind of new thought. Nonetheless, her excitement was returning and she began to think of her journey as being extremely blessed of God and extremely relevant to the contemporary world.

"Only just be patient," she would tell herself. It was hard to be pa-tient. Ron Giese continued to be her maven. They spent hours in his office in dialogue over the veiled meanings of some of the Hebrew words that Jana could see as possible answers to her deepest queries.

"Ron, let's take another look at what could have really happened in Genesis 1. When viewed under the scrutiny of the original language, new and incredibly marvelous ideas begin to surface. Recall that these are *ideas* that will have to be tested and nurtured and studied over time before they become theory or theology."

Ron was interested. Jana continued excitedly.

"Look at Genesis 1. A verbal tapestry is woven. This is not a static account of a historical event. This is a dynamic and moving tale of great action and motion. Try not to understand the words as just words. Try to understand them as if they were music. There are crescendos and decrescendos and accelerandos and ritardandos. The word *qara*—"to cry out"—has a much deeper, sharper color than the word *rachaph*—"to grow soft, relax, flutter." The colors are limitless, and if one were to, in his sanctified imagination, transfer those colors into sound, the depth, richness, and multiplicity of that sound would make the most complex fugue of Johannes Sebastian Bach seem primitive. The profundity of the Beethoven *Missa Solemnis* would be as a simple folk tune. The account of Creation in the book of Genesis is a thrilling, moving, and musically suitable account."

Ron was always supportive, as was Claude. But Ron withheld explicit commentary in favor of just helping Jana to think. Later, Jana would recall that however reserved he was, Ron never criticized anything that she said. She took that as implicit agreement. Occasionally, he would say something like, "Keep that thought and you might record it in your notes. Good thinking."

The word *rachaph* held a special intrigue for Jana. She reacted to the word as a singer, of course, would react. In its most simple verb form the word would be translated as "to grow soft, to relax."

"Aha!" Jana mused. "Just as a singer must allow the entire organism, the entire body to grow soft and relaxed before taking in that pre-emptive breath—that breath which energizes the whole beautiful sound which is singing—if the body is not relaxed, then the life-giving breath cannot penetrate the entire body in order to engage all of the resonators."

Jana knew well that "breathing" for the singer did not just mean to inhale. It meant to take in life-providing air which could engage every core cell of the singing instrument—the body—and without it, the sound would decay before it started.

"What a magnificent depiction of the life-giving breath of the Holy Spirit as it permeates our spirits and fills us with eternal vitality, life, and song. There is a connection here."

Jana would then recall the magnificence of the Mohler organ at West Point. Without its bellows which filled its being with enlivening air, there would have been no sound. And no music.

Gradually, over a period of months, an image began to form in Jana's sanctified imagination. She could imagine, intuit, if you please, the Omnipotent God hovering over the deep, becoming relaxed, flaccid, in the sense of complete relaxation, as one commentator phrased it, and then lovingly, deliberately taking in that infinite, immense, immeasurable breath of eternal proportions, pausing for one great moment of focusing and centering His entire Omniscient Being, and then finally uttering that unutterable Song—the Song of Creation.

It certainly was not that Jana was ascribing human characteristics of any sort to the Almighty God. Rather, it was quite the opposite. She could easily understand that our propensity for beauty and for the singing of songs in the most beautiful way came from God Himself, Who gave us that gift as a very dim representation of His magnificent singing.

Vivid as her imagination was, she could not even begin to frame the magnitude and beauty of that song, or the immensity of the Creation that it was framing. All she could perceive in her mind's eye was the absolute and inconceivable beauty and order that was demanded by that Song. The "beauty of holiness"? Maybe.

But the essence of that Eternal Song sung by the Eternal God, as Jana intuited it, was, in fact the most unutterably stunning sound which flung the galaxies into space and the planets into their orbits. No wonder the aurora sang; no wonder the very mountains and hills and stars and rocks and trees were commanded later on to raise their voices in song and their hands in clapping the joyous rhythm of the Creation alive and moving through space.

188

Jana knew well that incredible freedom when the voice is activated and beautiful song issues forth. It took her whole body to accomplish just a few bars of beautiful sound; then another intake of life-energizing breath to make another phrase—and on and on the song would go—out into eternity, Shaw said. Never ending and always living and always singing.

A moment in timeless time, for there was no time in the beginning. But the Word of God says so clearly "in the beginning" and that is when time was put in place for man to understand. This was Jana's glorious image of the Creation Song.

Thoughts would spin almost out of control in Jana's mind, all at once.

Robert Shaw: "Make that first sound perfect. It will go on forever."

Bill Dalglish: "The man that hath no music in his soul—I would be no such man."

The Old Testament itself would crash back into her memory: "Sing for joy, O heavens, for the Lord has done this; shout aloud, O earth beneath. Burst into song, you mountains, you forests and all your trees, for the Lord has redeemed Jacob, he displays his glory in Israel."

But one thought reigned in her mind. The Singing God. Jana had no proof that God sang until one day when she found the following verse, Zephaniah 3:17 (NIV):

"The Lord your God is with you, he is mighty to save. He will take great delight in you, he will quiet you with his love, he will *rejoice over you with singing.*"

"There it is," Jana was exultant. "Zephaniah has recorded that our God sings!"

Chapter 44

MODULATION: A MODAL CHANGE

Many Hebrew verbs in Genesis fascinated Jana. *Bara* was used to signify created, but only when God was the subject. *Amar* could mean to say, speak or utter. *Qara* could variously be translated as to cry out, to call, to call the name of God, or to utter a loud sound. *Nathan* could mean to set, entrust, give, bestow or utter. *Dabar* among its other meanings translates to sing or to utter. Jana was amazed at the many Hebrew ways of expressing the English word *utter*. This was especially intriguing because the fact that these concepts were capable of moving easily from speaking to *uttering* to singing harmonized with her own theory.

Since the word *amar* translates "to speak" or "to utter," one has to ask the question: can *amar*, by inference then, also be understood to mean "to sing" because one of its primary translations is "to utter" as well as "to speak"? So far, there is no concrete evidence that it can; but there is also no evidence that it cannot, either. Jana was not intimidated by the lack of research evidence on the subject. Her sacred imaginations had stood her in good stead down

through the years, and she believed that this intuition would come to fruition in due time.

Jana made a study of these Hebrew verbs and her ideas concerning them and discussed them with Dr. Giese:

- **Genesis 1:1:** *"created"—"bara":* to be made with God (always) as the subject.

- **Genesis 1:2:** *"hovered"—"rachaph":* to grow soft, relax, flutter (to become flaccid).

- **Genesis 1:3:** *"said"—"amar":* to say, speak, *utter.*

- **Genesis 1:3:** *"said"—"anah": to utter tunefully.* (Jana found another intuitive connection between these two verbs: *amar and anah.* The idea of *"uttering"* in English bound them together. It was an idea she could not get out of her head.)

- **Genesis 1:5:** *"called"—"qara":* to cry out, *utter* a loud sound, to call with the name of God

- **Genesis 1:17:** *"set"—"nathan":* to set, to entrust, give, bestow, to *utter.*

Ron Giese agreed with Jana that the Hebrew language was unique in that it had a beautifully living quality about it. It certainly was not, he would admit, a static language. Its capacity for vitality and expansiveness was limitless.

Vagrant thoughts. But they did connect. And again it was the musicality of the thought that intrigued Jana. And Hebrew was, if nothing else, a musical language.

Chapter 45

HOCKET: SIXTEENTH CENTURY

ne day after Hebrew class, Dr. Giese asked Jana if she had ever read anything about parallelism in Hebrew literature or poetry. She had not.

"Here are a couple of books on Hebrew poetry, Jana. Take them home and read them. If you have any questions, e-mail me or bring them to class and if I have a few minutes, I will talk them over with you."

Ron was always helpful and interested. It was so refreshing, because Jana had had so many years of frustrating "aloneness" in her quest. It was a pleasant release from the conflict and instability of the last decade or so. She took the books home and started to read. But not for long. The first few pages of one of the books triggered a thought about a scripture she had found a while back. Job 38 was the account of God's conversation with Job as He challenged Job to consider Who He was, in fact, and what Job's relationship should be to Him. Jana made a study of the scripture in the book of Job, and then wrote the following excerpt:

"Job is obviously being challenged by his God. God wants to know what Job is thinking about the earth and its foundations."

In her sanctified imagination, Jana can see Job asking the same questions that she is asking: "How did you create all this, God? What were your tools and building blocks? What happened at the moment when you said '—and let there be—'"

God indulgently answered:

> *"Where were you when I laid the foundations of the earth?*
>
> *Tell, Me, if you have understanding.*
>
> *Who determined its measurements?*
>
> *Surely you know!*
>
> *Or, who stretched the line upon it?*
>
> *To what were its foundations fastened?*
>
> *Or who laid its cornerstone,*
>
> *When the morning stars sang together,*
>
> *And all the sons of God shouted for joy?"*

"Therefore I have uttered what I did not understand. Things too wonderful for me, which I did not know."[vi] This reply echoed Jana's thoughts accurately.

[vi] Job 42:2,3b (NKJV)

Chapter 45

When God asked Job, "To what were the foundations (of the world and the universe) fastened?" He was asking the ultimate question. And in the next two statements, He was, in sanctified imagination, giving us a marvelous clue to the answer. God says (sings), "When the morning stars *sang* together, And all the sons of God *shouted* for joy..."

Two things caught Jana's interest. First, the words "sang" and "shouted." Over and over again, the scriptures use these two words in confluence. Jana recalled that Ron had told her that parallelism is a powerful poetic and syntactical instrument in Hebrew poetry and in the Hebrew Scriptures. Job 38:7 (NKJV) is an outstanding example:

> *"When the morning stars* sang *together,*
>
> *And all the sons of God* shouted *for joy"*
>
> *Isaiah 42:11 (NKJV) uses the same technique:*
> *"Let the inhabitants of the rock* sing,
>
> *Let them* shout *from the top of the mountains."*
>
> *Again in Zephaniah 3:14 (NKJV):*
> "Sing, *O daughter of Zion!*
>
> Shout, *O Israel!"*

Literally, there is a flowing together, a confluence, of two streams of thought in the very use of these words. There seems to be, at least in a poetic sense, a very close relationship between these words in that they are used in the same verses to say the same thing: Give praise to Almighty God!

195

"Singing" and "shouting" and "speaking" and "saying" *seem* to be locked together in meaning and *seem* to have all to do with the creative process when "God laid the foundations of the earth." Much of the clarity of this thought is lost in our present-day language and biblical translations, but even cursory research into the vast richness of the language of the Old Testament exposes a wealth of information which is veiled in our vernacular. It must also be remembered that the Hebrew language is an intuitive language and can only be understood as it is allowed to have life and breath. Context is vital and the order in which words are arranged becomes vital as well. It is artistic and expressive beyond simple syntactical excellence.

Therefore it is of great importance that we ask the following question: Why is it that the phrases "singing together" and "shouting for joy" are so intimately placed in this scripture along with the idea of the cohesive power holding the foundations of the earth together? Could it be that *that* cohesive power is *music*—but not our music? Rather, could it be the music of God as He speaks and sings to His Creation?

What did God say to Job: "Tell me, *if you have understanding.*"

The real nugget of truth to be seen here is the phrase: "To what were its foundations fastened?"

Jana was interested to find that the creative process, when "God laid the foundations of the earth," seemed in the Hebrew to be closely linked with sounds—singing, shouting, speaking—although this was somewhat lost in English versions. What is the cohesive power to which the earth's foundations were fastened?

Jana pondered, she wondered, could this power be music? In a manner of speaking, did God perhaps *sing* the universe into existence? Because we do know that God sings, don't we?

Chapter 46

THEME III: COUNTERSUBJECT OF A FUGUE
SCIENCE CONCURS? BUT, OF COURSE.

ana's thoughts were undergoing a shift. She was beginning to muse over the place that science would take in her theories, or even if science would tolerate being billed with religion as it existed in the twentieth and twenty-first centuries. She knew very little, if anything, about quantum physics, for instance, but now and again there would be an article in the Wall Street Journal or the Investor's Business Daily that Jack subscribed to which would address some of the newest findings of science concerning the conflict between evolution and creationism. Most of the media accounts leaned very clearly to the "irrefutable" position of the evolutionist and his theories. But even reading those accounts fertilized Jana's thinking, even if she disagreed vociferously with them. And then, there was the question about the origins of matter, which figured into the theories of both evolution and creationism.

Jana made no apology for her position: she took the position of believing in first cause along with St. Thomas Aquinas and felt that it was not in the domain of her present work to try to prove or disprove Aquinas' claims—or

evolution's, for that matter. Her main interest was in the actual moment of Creation. And there was ample room for discussion just on that one point without furthering the debate with rabbit trails.

Somewhere along the way at about this time, Jana rediscovered the article written by Edward Rothstein entitled, "Math and Music: The Deeper Links." She reviewed the article eagerly. It appeared that there were many highly intellectual people out there who were chasing the same vague idea that there was a magnificent interconnection that provided some reasonable logic to trying to solve the dilemma: how do things relate or do they? Apparently they do relate, or else people like Edward Rothstein would not take the time nor spend the energy to "relate" music to math and try to develop the relationship between the two and even go so far as to say that these two very diametrically opposed disciplines give us "reshaped" understanding of our reality as creatures of the universe.

One of the interesting concepts that Rothstein discussed was that it was easy for musicians to invoke mathematical precepts to describe the orderliness of their art. But it may be a bit more evasive to ascribe artistic attributes to the "science" of mathematics.

However, "mathematicians and physicists of all epochs have felt (the) affinities" between the two disciplines. Didn't Galileo speculate about the "numerical reasons" for some tones being more pleasing than others? Euclid joined the discussion nearly 2,000 years later. In the eighteenth century, Euler wrote a comprehensive paper on the relationship of consonance (musical, and by inference consonance in other venues) to whole numbers. The body of interwoven information grew and grew. Johannes Kepler finally made the astounding assumption that the very movements of the planets created a "music of the spheres"—a sonic counterpart to his mathematical laws of planetary motion.

Chapter 46

The underlying strength of reason is found in the earliest writings of men such as Plato, Aristotle, and Pythagoras. Jana reflected that perhaps the Greeks had a much keener understanding of the relationships and connections among disciplines than modern man has. But it seemed to Jana that the further man travelled on his journey of building knowledge, the less impact was imparted by the doctrines of the early Greeks.

To add to the growing instability of Jana's situation intellectually and emotionally as time went by was the growing awareness that these were ideas that most of her peers, and certainly her immediate family, were either unwilling or unable to discuss with her. She began to feel very isolated. She had no way to judge her own worth. Time went on and she continued to think.

She went to her pastor with musical issues pertaining to the decadence of music in the church at large. He did not understand and did not, apparently, have the time to devote to her issues. She was suffering from increasing doubt about her spiritual acuity. Maybe God did not give her this insight. Maybe her "sanctified imagination" was just too big, like her imaginary pilot friends of decades ago.

Providential intervention always astounded Jana. Just when things seemed the most confounding, an answer would often surface.

Chapter 47

FUGAL ANSWER: AUGMENTATION:
SUBJECT RE-ITERATED IN DOUBLED NOTE VALUES

It was a Sunday evening, and Jana and Jack were watching TV. Jack was involved in his customary male channel surfing activities. He flicked on the local public television station. A voice said something like:

"And the scientists from Columbia University and Cambridge, UK, are exploring this exciting idea that the most fundamental particle of matter will ultimately be proven to be nothing more than an infinitesimal 'string' of vibrating energy, along with a team of worldwide scientists who call themselves the 'string theorists.'"

There was a graphic of a guitar on the screen.

"Stop, Jack! Stop! That's it!! That's it!! We have to listen! That's it!"

The engineer's mind, in its own pragmatic way, must go through a checklist of "what it is" that we are talking about before it can react. Jack was not agitated, he just sounded agitated.

"What's *it?* What *it* are we talking about? What did you hear that was so world-stopping?"

Jana was so excited that she was not being particularly articulate. Almost instantaneously, Jana intuited that she had just been given the answer. Somehow she knew that this "string theory" was going to provide her with the bridge she so desperately needed to move from her familiar and beloved artistic world into the world that was so mysteriously foreign to her, but so very necessary to give credence to her world—the world of science was giving her a gift of understanding.

About that time, a youngish man came on camera. It was Brian Greene, himself. He looked more like a college senior than one of the foremost experimental scientists in the world. His style was direct, articulate, and even amusing.

Jana heard him saying that this new theory, with its earliest roots dating from the mid-twentieth century, allows that the smallest, most infinitesimal particle of matter is nothing more, and nothing less, than strings of vibrating energy! He said that what he was trying to explain may turn out to be the unifying theory of everything in the cosmos.

Vibrating strings of energy. The essence of song! Vibrating energy!

Her mind flew back to Robert Shaw: "The sound never stops—it is part of the cosmos."

Joseph Flummerfelt: "The essence of song is vibrating energy."

Marvin Keenze: "The whole body is set to vibrating and the resonators, though primarily in your cranial cavities, involve your entire body."

Vibrating energy!

Jana was mesmerized as she continued to listen to the young scientist expound his theories and discoveries, and she sensed that it was the

beginning of a new phase for her. Resolution and the return of stability—reconciliation—could not be far away. This had to be the answer that she had been in quest of for so long. But the conflict was not over yet. This new idea of hers was more eccentric than any of the others. Her peers, though interested, were not excited. They offered her a charitable acceptance. Some of them even mused that it may be worth further study. She was so grateful for Ron Giese at that point, because he seemed to be the only one besides her husband who could say with any conviction that he thought her theory was valid.

Although Brian Greene did not invent this "string theory," he quickly became one of the main proponents of it through his book and the television documentaries based on it. Standing in front of a screen with the image of a guitar displayed on it, Greene said:

"The building blocks of reality, as it appears to us, are merely a pattern of their vibrations, just as strings on a guitar vibrate at different rates to produce different notes. If true (and string theory has never been *experimentally* tested) the theory would be the unified, overarching explanation of how the universe works—the solution that physicists from Isaac Newton to Albert Einstein have been seeking for centuries."[vii]

Jana bought *The Elegant Universe* and several other books by such scholars as Stephen Hawking, the renowned physicist who still holds the Lucasian Professor of Mathematics chair at Cambridge University. This is the post that was held by Isaac Newton in 1669. She subscribed to *Scientific American* and several other journals and began a two year study of "string theory" and the "theory of everything" as first proposed by Albert Einstein. She was not prepared for the incredible things she would learn as a result of her studies. Being a typically myopic student whose main

---

[vii] These quotations are actually from an interview with Brian Braiker of *Newsweek*: March 26, 2004: They contain the essential information that so changed Jana's emphasis in thinking.

interest was music, she had always been grateful that she had learned to fly. That had opened new vistas to Jana that were mind-boggling enough, but, now, she was entering the halls of a technical discipline that she had never even considered as being available to her because of her almost total "right-brained" intellect. It had been implied to her all her life that the "creative mind" was woefully limited and challenged in its ability to grasp things of scientific and technical bent. Not that she agreed, but…

So here it was. Again, her intuitive nature took on the challenge of believing that the answer to centuries of quest lay in the uncovering of the fact that the greatest physicists of the age were entertaining the theory that all matter was made up of nothing but "vibrating strings." Therefore, there could be growing credibility in her theory that when Creation was achieved, it was by the means of musical elements. This also gave growing credibility to the position of the creationists who claimed that the act of creation was centered in the power of God; to the Intelligent Design camp who could not go all the way to the Bible for credibility but could accept the idea of a "Higher Power" who was the Grand Designer; and it even lent a certain new interest to the idea of the "big bang," because it could agree with the contention of the proponents of that theory that there was, indeed, a moment of tremendous expenditure of energetic release from a compacted density which could not be explained by their own calculations.

Jana and Jack had missed almost half of this first installment of the Nova production of "The Elegant Universe," a three part television documentary based on Greene's book by the same name. But, no matter, this was only the introductory segment of what proved to be pivotal for Jana in dealing with her "transient half-ideas" with which she had been grappling for so many years. What he said was especially intriguing, coming from a physicist of his stature:

"Integrating the discoveries of physics into our collective world-view is a slow process. Even today, nearly a century after Einstein, most people have yet to appreciate fully the experimentally confirmed lessons coming from Einstein or those of the quantum. By fearlessly taking on the science, and leveraging its intrinsic fascination to produce entertaining works of substance and drama, the arts may well be the perfect medium to fully integrate science into the world's conversation."[viii]

It went through Jana's mind that this statement put the "cart before the horse" by making the inference that the arts could be the medium of integration of understanding when she felt, intuitively, that the arts, and especially music, were the actual *origins*, somehow, of all other manifestations of universal cohesion and not any sort of resultant communicative-creative activity. But, right now, this was such a magnificent example of Shaw's "transient half-idea" that Jana knew it was futile to try to give it any further shape just yet. She also knew that she would have to learn much more about this string theory in order to be intelligent about expressing her ideas.

The discovery of string theory was a turning point, indeed, for Jana. It was the beginning of an intensive two years of self-education during which time she studied Einstein and his quest for the theory of everything and realized that the theory of relativity had very far-reaching ramifications, indeed.

This new knowledge of things scientific astounded Jana. She had always steered clear of such pursuits because they seemed too inaccessible for her. She should have known better. The more she studied, the more excited she became about this new turn of interest. Getting to know men like Michio Kaku through his writings and TV documentaries was

[viii] *The Elegant Universe:* Brian Greene: W.W. Norton & Company, Inc.:1999:Preface:Pg. ix

exhilarating. And everything that Jana learned from these great scientists gave her ammunition for her own developing theory:

- **Gabriele Veneziano:** "String theory is the leading (though not only) theory that tries to describe what happened at the moment of the big bang. The strings that the theory describes are material objects much like those on a violin. As violinists move their fingers down the neck of the instrument, they shorten the strings and increase the frequency (hence energy) of their vibrations. If they reduced a string to a sub-subatomic length, quantum effects would take over and prevent it from being shortened any further. How can such a simple-minded theory describe the complicated world of particles and their interactions? The answer can be found in what we may call quantum string magic. Once the rules of quantum mechanics are applied to a vibrating string—just like a miniature violin string, except that the vibrations propagate along it at the speed of light—new properties appear. All have profound implications for particle physics and cosmology."[ix]

- **Edward Witten:** "Just like the beauty of music, so the richness of the string comes from the fact that the string can vibrate in many different ways."[x]

[ix] *Scientific American: The Myth of the Beginning of Time:* Gabriele Veneziano: May 2004

[x] http://www.thirteen.org/bigideas/witten.html

- **Michio Kaku:** "Pluck a string on a guitar and you hear a single note. Pluck a different string and, because the strings vibrate at different frequencies, you hear a different note. Combine strings and you get chords. By combining the five strings of a guitar and causing them to vibrate at different frequencies, a musician can create infinitude of musical structure."[xi]

- **Brian Greene:** "We will take strings to be nature's most fundamental ingredient. It requires no input beyond a single number. That sets the benchmark scale for measurements. All properties of the micro world are within the realm of its explanatory power. To understand this, let's first think about more familiar strings, such as those on a violin. Each such string can undergo a huge variety…of different vibrational patterns known as resonances. These are the wave patterns whose peaks and troughs are evenly spaced and fit perfectly between the string's two fixed endpoints. Our ears sense these different resonant vibrational patterns as different musical notes. The strings in string theory have similar properties. There are resonant vibrational patterns that the string can support by virtue of their evenly spaced peaks and troughs exactly fitting along its special extent. Just as the different vibrational patterns of a violin string give rise to different musical notes, the different vi-

---

[xi] http://www.msnbc.com/news/201650.asp?cpl=1

brational patterns of a fundamental string give rise to different masses and force changes. This overview shows how string theory offers a truly wonderful unifying framework. Every particle of matter and every transmitter of force consists of a string whose pattern of vibration is its 'fingerprint'."

- **Brian Greene:** "Because every physical event, process, or occurrence in the universe is, at its most elementary level, describable in terms of forces acting between these elementary material constituents, string theory provides the promise of a single, all inclusive, unified description of the physical universe: a theory of everything."[xii]

The very structure of the universe, Jana believed, contained its own validation, and this validation was increasingly being supported by contemporary scientific investigation.

Jana mused, "The concept of space, time, and matter—the very center of the contemplations about our universe—is a Trinitarian concept."

Her musician's mind flew to the construct of Western music. "A triadic system, in which a triad contains three tones, each a third apart, *could* also describe the Trinitarian concept. Music and things musical were evident at every turn. Transient half-ideas. Hmmm."

"Remember Robert Shaw's transient half-ideas, and do not jump to the conclusion that this idea is fallacious," Jana thought. "After all,

[xii] *The Elegant Universe:* Brian Greene: W.W. Norton & Company, Inc.:1999:Pgs. 142,143,146.

even the great minds of the scientific world are not dogmatic about the existence of 'strings,' but they probably do have enough corroboration to validate them. As James Burke said, 'As the body of knowledge changes, so do we' and the body of knowledge is under a great deal of change right now."

As she pondered the new knowledge gleaned over the past year or so, Jana recalled that Einstein had speculated extensively about the rift between the macro world of relativity which dealt with the huge issues of the universe—planets, orbits, light years—and the micro world of quantum physics which dealt with the infinitesimal issues of the universe—atoms, electrons, and photons. The macro world was huge and, in a sense, placid and orderly. It moved according to strict laws and could be considered to be predictable. The micro world, on the other hand, was frenetic and full of what seemed to be unceasing and inestimable activity. On the face of it, there seemed to be no way of reconciliation of the two—that is, until string theory made its entrance.

In 1997, a scientist in Tokyo made the comparison: "The energy 'uncertainty' introduced in quantum theory combines with the 'mass-energy equivalence' of special relativity…"

This comparison stated in just a few words the quandary that was causing a great deal of agreement and disagreement among scientists, Jana discovered. But another of those startling half-ideas launched itself into her brain as she thought about the dichotomy between the two. What, after all, was the big discrepancy? Another musical analogy formed itself unbidden in her mind.

"Think of the symphony orchestra, poised on the stage to perform the magnificent Beethoven Ninth Symphony. The altogether anchored and weighty sonorities of that great symphonic work have been one of

the bulwarks of musical and intellectual understanding for almost 200 years. The ultimate peace and yet exhilaration of the fourth movement has qualified it to become the Anthem of Europe in the twentieth century. Certainly, energy equivalence is one of the hallmarks of this work, with its balance and unequivocal steadfast expression."

On the other hand, Jana mused, "There is without question a demanding energy uncertainty in the activity of the orchestra in its tuning phase. The most minute of frequency adjustments and compensations is taking place in every single one of the eighty-odd instruments on the stage and every single musician is frenetically attempting to bring perfect sound into play as he tunes his particular instrument to the split-hundredth of a vibration per second. Could that portray the differences in the relativity and quantum worlds, at least in the sacred imaginations of people who understand the idea of extended thought?"

Jana was more sure than ever that the "sphered thought" would fit into the "cubed suit" because it would grow corners, as Shaw had predicted. She knew that her theory was taking wings.

There was one last enigma. The "big bang." Science has by this time fairly well proven that there was, indeed, a point in time when something cataclysmic did happen. Some enormous burst of enormous energy from some enormously dense source energetically flung the worlds and galaxies and universes out into the cosmos and energized them to maintain their flight.

Of course, science, up to now, had not been able to really quantify or qualify that moment, merely calling it the "big bang." Jana knew the immense intake of life-giving breath into a relaxed body, the focused engagement of the body, and the deliberate and beautiful exhalation of

that life-giving breath that made it possible to fill the Westminster Chapel with song during one's vocal recital just before graduation. What if that action epitomized the moment in unrecorded time because there was no time when the Almighty God made the very first audible sound of temporal eons and sang Creation into being? Wouldn't that have caused some sort of cataclysmic event? Couldn't that event have been totally musical in essence? Of course!

Chapter 48

LINEAR HARMONY: MELODY PREEMPTS TRADITION

here were many other events and contacts that enabled Jana along her way and as time moved forward, she became more and more settled in her quest. She was grateful for the new sense of direction and confidence.

Two volumes became Jana's textbooks in her quest to reconcile the scientific with the artistic and theological. And she was beginning to think that to divorce the artistic from the theological was a non sequitur.

Jana was astute enough to realize that she was dealing with at least two very pressing considerations, and that on the surface, they seemed to have absolutely nothing to do with one another. In fact, they seemed, on the surface, to be diametrically opposed. One was scientific in nature and involved the beginnings of things and the relationships of things from the point of view of the physicist. It dealt with ratios, theorems, formulae, and quantum mechanics. But that did not deter her.

The other problem was more personal, because it was theological and musical in nature and dealt with two of the disciplines most beloved to

213

Jana—her faith and her music. Although she had never articulated, even to herself, how these two schools of knowledge were related, she felt intuitively that they were practically inseparable. In fact, it was beginning to become quite clear in her sanctified imagination that the answer lay in melding these two fields of knowledge, and that was becoming more feasible as the months went by.

Expressing these ideas, which were less and less acceptable as "half-ideas," in a way that would grip her peers and readers was the only real quandary left. All she needed was a forum.

The pieces of the puzzle were falling into place. Jana was grateful for the wild imagination of the little girl of ten who hung on to life so tenaciously and who dared to seek and find excitement in her musical forays. That quality of belief in the world beyond, where beauty and truth lived in harmony stood her in good stead and actually provided a bed-rock for her intuitions. What she saw in her sanctified imagination seldom, if ever, conflicted with that truth. Her faith in God was also instinctive and she was grateful for that. Her Christian education was strong and she was grateful for that.

And so Jana continued to read and study and to correspond with as many scholars as she could influence to hear her out concerning her theories and ideas—and half-ideas. None of them were discouraging to her; they may not have been deeply involved in her developing ideas, but they were not discouraging to her. They urged her to keep thinking and writing.

It was, by this time, the spring of 2010.

Chapter 49

CODA: BY DEFINITION

A fter the final cadence of the recapitulation, the movement may continue into a "tail," which will contain material from the movement proper. Codas, when present, vary considerably in length, but, like introductions, are not part of the "argument" of the work, however it ends with a perfect cadence in the home key. Codas may be quite brief end-pieces, or they may be very long and elaborate; a famous example is the finale of Beethoven's Eighth Symphony.

Jana mused over the first movement of the Beethoven's *Pathetique Sonata*. It had been one of the works that her children had loved to hear her play during their early years when the family lived in the church parlors in Mount Morris, New York, where their father had a small pastorate. For someone who does not know the work, she thought, it would be very difficult to explain it—words, again, simply fail in the uttering. But to hear it played

embodies all of the pathos of life itself—anxiety, perhaps even anger, yearning, determination—it is all there in the first movement. But the remarkable thing is that the entire opening two pages are recapitulated completely in three lines, fifteen measures, at the very end in the *coda*.

"Here I am," Jana looked out into the distance where the blue hills of Virginia merged into the bluer sky. "Now I must condense sixty-eight years into three lines, fifteen measures, and make sense of the whole thing. Where to start?"

Jana answered her own question.

"I shall simply tell you what I believe as a result of living my life as I have and learning the things I have learned. This is what I believe. This is the coda to my sonata."

Before I continue with my coda, I must make one thing clear. Jana is, in a way, my alter-ego. Now I must let her go, because she has served me so well in allowing me to tell the story of my life without being too intimately involved in the process. She will always be such a good friend, because she could express things I may have personally found too difficult. But now the raison d'etre for Jana, and for me, is to tell you, the readers, what it is that we both believe so intensely and for that, I must be myself.

The driving force behind me, even before I knew quite what it was that I was searching for, started when I was still a child. Having survived a terrible illness as a ten-year-old because of a piece of music written by Johannes Brahms, I was the personal recipient of the healing power of music. Growing up in a family fraught with financial and health problems brought tremendous stress and sadness into our world, and it was always the wonder of music that transported me to a world where I could feel safe.

It was a piece of music written by my first real piano teacher that was an emotional mainstay for me in an eighteen-year marriage also filled with sadness and fear. Such is the foundation for a life-long quest for what later I began to call *truth in music*. The result of that quest is a hypothesis that has been slowly composed and orchestrated mostly in spite of me by a loving God Who has walked beside me these "forty years in the wilderness" as He did with the Israelites of old. This is the hypothesis which I am extending in the hope that it will become a theory to be considered.

Chapter 50

CODA: OR IS IT CREDO?

$\mathcal{I}$ very often quote one of the scholars whom I most respect because he put into one statement the entirety of the quest which has identified my life. Dr. Jeremy Begbie stated: "It is clear *that* music is one of the most powerful communicative media we have, but *how* it communicates and *what* it communicates are anything but clear."

I happened on this quote from his wonderful book, *Theology, Music and Time,* many years into my quest for truth in music.. It crystallized my thinking and enabled me to begin forging the final shape of my thesis. It never made sense to me that musicians of all kinds and in all stages of training and ability were so unable to describe what it was about their art that set it so far above any other art form. The nomenclature given to music—"the universal language"—always seemed to be a somewhat trite bow to the overarching power of music, but it certainly did not satisfy my need to know why it had this power.

Of course, there was my own classical training as a young pianist which only served to deepen my yearning to understand. It was not until I finally

found myself in Westminster Choir College as a mature woman that I had my first insight into the real depth of influence that music holds over all of creation. It was the general respect given to the wondrous sacred choral masterpieces and the performances I was privileged to be part of that made me begin to understand that there was a power much beyond the music itself that held things in such perfect tension and gave so much incontrovertible beauty to this otherwise sterile and sinful world. There was real release in that music and I had to know why.

That the power was eternal and sacred was no problem to me. It was trying to understand why that kept me struggling forward off and on throughout my mature years. Attempts to find support for my thinking and help in forging my theory were futile. There was no literature in the research libraries, and most of my colleagues were puzzled by my refusal to accept "the gift" of my talent at face value and just enjoy it. I intuited that there was so much more to it than that. And, of course, then Robert Shaw came into my sphere of learning with his incredible philosophical and theological acuity and began to teach us about truth in music.

"Truth is truth," he would say, "and if you find it in the music as you should, you are greatly blessed."

The greatest impact that this seed of thought planted in my brain was the performance of the Beethoven *Missa Solemnis* where Shaw taught us to hear the hammer blows against the cross in the Crucifixus.

But no one was able to agree openly with me that the power of music had anything to do with God. That He gave gifts of talent and ability to a select few, yes, but that His character and Spirit lay at the root of what the music was, no. There were "good" reasons for that from the human point of view, shaped by human logic. That being the case, how then could you explain acid rock? Or the drug culture that follows such genre? What about pagan drumming? What about the myriads of arguments that could be formulated to support any one or any dozen of preferences out there?

Also, I had to cope with the entirety of creation and knowledge. One would have to be rather opaque in one's thinking to deny that music infiltrates every phase of life from the birds' songs to the winds' murmurings to the aurora's whistles to the rhythmic cycles of all of life. Musical metaphors and analogies cannot be escaped. Why?

Then, there is the obvious presence of something cohesive in all of creation. There are parallels that can be drawn between any disciplines or fields of knowledge. That triggers the thought of the poetic device in the Hebrew language called parallelism—what is it and why does it exist? It began to dawn on me as I neared my sixth decade that it is not accidental that all of these "parallels" are so predictable in our universe—the universe of the mind, of the world, and of the spirit. But how to delineate what I was thinking? How to shape it into a viable theory that could be tried and found to be wanting or *found to be truth?*

The beginnings of an answer came in the form of *string theory.* As a youngster, I was taught that the smallest particle of matter was the atom—but then they split the atom. What then? It was a terrific moment of clarity when I first heard about string theory. Remember, string theory states, simply, that the most fundamental particles of matter are, no more or less than, infinitesimal "strings of vibrating energy." Vibrating energy! That is the quintessence of song. The essence of music! Vibrating energy—the building blocks of the universe and of all creation! Amazing!

I was, by the time I got my introduction to this theory of the physics of matter, in my early seventies. It was a moment when the kaleidoscopic events of my intellectual life suddenly snapped into focus like an old-fashioned slide in the hot beam of a projector when the heat caused it to

abruptly find its own sharp image on the screen. Of course! What if God did not simply speak the words "—and let there be—"? What if He, the Singing God of Zephaniah, sang those commands?

The knowledge that the Hebrew language may give rise to this idea came slowly over the three or so years that I studied with Dr. Giese. Again, it was very difficult to find a Hebrew scholar who would be willing to tackle the idea that the Hebrew verbs may supply such latitude, but on the other hand, none of them with whom I conferred contradicted me or suggested that I abandon my search. All encouraged me to keep thinking and keep learning and keep writing. And so I did.

The core of this hypothesis lies in the understanding of what the Creation drama really was and how it occurred. Grasping this concept would answer many age-old questions, not the least of which is what *is* drama anyway and why does every culture have its dramatic folklore and traditions? This is precisely the point at which the emerging discipline of performance criticism enters and opens volumes of new insight into the process of cultural development and cohesiveness. And drama infers the presence of all art, as Richard Wagner made so clear in his massive operatic masterpieces. The entire saga of the artistic world could be clarified if we could begin to grasp the idea that all of life, knowledge, and creation *is* musical in nature by virtue of its very created building blocks. At this point, the secular world has provided the final essential piece of the puzzle, I believe.

Science, in the name of string theory, is now saying that the very elements of matter that comprise the created world and the very glue that holds it all together, is vibrating energy. What if that energy is the singing energy of Very God? What if He, indeed, did not merely speak the universes into being, but actually definitively *sang* them into being?

Chapter 50

Scripture tells us clearly that it is the Word of God, Jesus Christ, that holds all things together. What if, in "parallelistic" fashion, that Word of God can be seen as "dabar"—the Song of God? The next step in the logic would be to understand that musical elements and entities are the very stuff of Creation and that, therefore, there is an eternality about music that can only be explained by acknowledging a singing act of God at the moment of Creation.

One of the most pivotal encounters in my entire quest was the opportunity to personally meet and speak with Dr. Begbie from Cambridge and to ask him more about his thinking on the communicative powers of music. The question arose immediately: how much am I willing to invest in pursuing the musical metaphor of God as the Singing Creator? Is there really any philosophical or theological support for attributing eternality to music because it has existed along with the eternality of God?

There is one massive caveat: this music about which we are concerned is not the music of human creation and cognition. This is what the music of man reflects just as it reflects—so very dimly—any other of the attributes of God.

Then there is this: we understand that our Omniscient God can be seen, among many other attributes, as Jehovah Jirah, El Shaddai, the Great Physician, God the Father, Son, and Holy Spirit. Could we not also begin to understand Him as the Singing Creator, the Singing God of Zephaniah 3:17? It is an idea that great thinkers have entertained before, C. S. Lewis and Tolkien among them. We could then answer the question of what it is and how it is that music communicates and that all of mankind can respond to that communication. *Truth in music is the voice of God singing to us and rejoicing over us with singing when we answer in faith.*

This is the end of the coda. But it is not the end of the story. Jana and I are 78 years young now and we still have work to do. And much more to learn. Maybe you, the readers, will join us.

Glossary

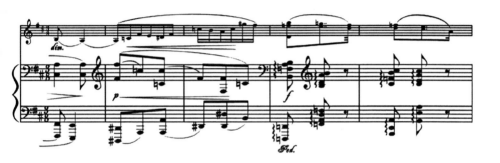

A Capella

In chapel style, without instrumental accompaniment; Italian, meaning to sing alone.

Accelerando

Gradually accelerating or getting faster. Abbreviated by accel.

Adagio

It., at ease. A slow tempo marking between Largo and Andante. A composition written in a slow tempo, frequently the second movement of sonatas, symphonies, etc.

AGITATO

A directive to perform the indicated passage in an agitated, hurried, or restless manner.

ALEATORY

Music in which the composer introduces the elements of chance or unpredictability with regard to either the composition or its performance.

ALLEGRO

A fast tempo marking between Allegretto and Vivace. A composition in fast tempo, especially the first and last movements of a sonata, symphony, etc.

ANACRUSTIC

Referring to an upbeat or pickup note(s); a term used for unstressed notes at the beginning of a phrase of music.

ARPEGGIO

It., A broken chord in which the individual notes are sounded one after the other instead of simultaneously. Playing the notes of a chord consecutively (harp style).

Glossary

ATTACA

A musical directive for the performer to begin the next movement (or section) of a composition immediately and without pause. This is common in classical literature. Attacca subito can also be used, with subito meaning suddenly or quickly. The terms are interchangeable.

AUGMENTATION

Statement of a melody in longer note values, often twice as slow as the original.

CADENCE

A stylized close in music which divides the music into periods or brings it to a full conclusion.

CADENZA

An ornamental passage performed near the close of a composition, usually improvised, and usually performed by a soloist. Cadenzas are mostly to be found in arias or concertos.

CANTABILE

Singing or performing in a melodious and graceful style, full of expression.

CANTARE

To sing, celebrate, or praise. Lat., to sing.

CANTUS FIRMUS

The basis of polyphonic compositions of the Middle Ages and Renaissance. The tune of the cantus firmus was taken from Gregorian chant; it would move very slowly underneath more rapid vocal or instrumental lines above it. A pre-existing melody forming the basis of a polyphonic composition. Lat., fixed melody.

CHACONNE

In music, a chaconne (Italian: ...*ciaconne)* [is a] fiery and suggestive dance that first appeared in Spain about 1600 AD and eventually gave its name to a musical form. Miguel de Cervantes, Francisco Gomez de Quevedo and other contemporary writers imply a Mexican origin but do not indicate whether it was indigenous or a Spanish dance modified there. Apparently danced with castanets by a couple or by a woman alone, it soon spread to Italy, where it was considered disreputable as it had been in Spain. During the 16th century, the dance became subdued and stylized, and in the 17th century it gained favor in the French court.... The musical form of the chaconne is a continuous variation (on some repeated short progression)." —Encyclopedia Britannica

228

Glossary

CODA

After the final cadence of the recapitulation, the movement may continue into a "tail," which will contain material from the movement proper. Codas, when present, vary considerably in length, but, like introductions, are not part of the "argument" of the work; however, it ends with a perfect cadence in the home key. Codas may be quite brief end-pieces, or they may be very long and elaborate; a famous example is the finale of Beethoven's Eighth Symphony.

COLORATURA

It., a soprano who sings elaborate ornamentation containing improvised or written out running passages and trills. This style was common in the 18th and 19th centuries in such arias as Wolfgang Amadeus Mozart's The Magic Flute Queen of the Night. These arias usually require a soprano with an extended high range. Also refers to the type of fluid, melismatic music usually sung by a coloratura soprano.

COUNTERPOINT

The art of combining two or more melodies to be performed simultaneously and musically. In counterpoint, the melody is supported by another melody rather than by chords.

COUNTERSUBJECT

The secondary theme of a fugue, heard against the subject. Also called a countertheme.

CRESCENDO

A directive to a performer to smoothly increase the volume of a particular phrase or passage.

CREDO

The third of the principal movements of the concert mass. Lat., means "I believe."

DA CAPO

A directive to the performer to go back to the beginning of the composition. This directive is abbreviated: D.C. It., from the top.

DIATONIC

Proceeding in the order of the octave based on five tones and two semitones. The major and natural minor scales and the modes are all diatonic. In the major scale, the semitones fall between the third and fourth tones and the seventh and eighth tones. In the minor scale, the semitones fall between the second and third tones and the fifth and sixth tones.

DIMINUENDO

It., diminishing. A directive to a performer to smoothly decrease the volume of the specific passage of a composition.

DIMINUTION

A Renaissance and Baroque ornamentation which consists of the restatement of a melody in which the note values are shortened, usually by half.

DIVINA PROPORTIONE: THE GOLDEN SECTION

The term Golden Section was given in the nineteenth century to the proportion derived from the division of a line into what Euclid (active about 300 BC) called "extreme and mean ratio." "A straight line," he explained, "is said to have been cut in extreme and mean ratio when, as the whole line is to the greater segment, so is the greater to the less." It is often claimed that the Golden Section is aesthetically superior to all other proportions, and, if it is admitted that what pleases the eye is unity in variety, it may be said that this proportion fulfills this condition better than any other.

DYNAMICS

The loudness or softness of a composition. The term piano (p) is used to indicate softness and forte (f) to indicate loudness.

ELISION

A musical situation in which the end of one pattern overlaps or coincides with the beginning of the next pattern. Overlapping maintains the motion of the phrase at cadence points and is used to weaken the cadence.

EPISODE

An element found in music that is a digression from the main structure of the composition. It is a passage that is not a part of the main theme groups of a composition, but is an ornamental or constructive section added to the main elements of the composition.

EXPOSITION

In sonata form, the exposition is the first statement of the theme; it is the first of the three major sections in sonata form. Usually there are two major theme groups in the exposition, possibly followed by a codetta. The exposition is followed by the development, in which the themes presented in the exposition are expanded, reshaped, and manipulated. Finally the same themes are presented in very nearly their original form in the recapitulation, which is the last section of the sonata form.

FORTE

A directive in music to perform a certain passage loudly. Forte is symbolized by the letter "f." It.

Glossary

FUGUE

A form of composition popular in, but not restricted to, the Baroque era, in which a theme or subject is introduced by one voice, and is imitated by other voices in succession. Usually only the first few notes of the subject are imitated exactly, then each voice deviates slightly until the next time it enters again with the subject. Generally the voices overlap and weave in and out of each other forming a continuous, tapestry-like texture.

GOLDEN MEAN

A ratio between two portions of a line or the two dimensions of a plane figure, in which the lesser of the two is to the greater as the greater is to the sum of both. A ratio of approximately 0.616 to 1.000. This ratio is artistically and acoustically inviolable.

GOLDEN RECTANGLE

A rectangular depiction of the Golden Mean or the Golden Section (Divina Proportione).

HARMONY

The combination of notes sounded simultaneously to produce chords. Usually, this term is used to describe consonance; however, it can also be used to describe dissonance.

HOCKET

A Medieval practice of composition in which two voices would move in such a manner that one would be still while the other moved and vice-versa. Sometimes this was achieved by taking a single melody and breaking it into short, one or two note phrases, and dividing the phrases between the two voices so that a quick back-and-forth movement of the melody would be heard.

INDETERMINACY

Indefinite or uncertain. Refers, in music, to some aspect of a composition that the composer places beyond his conscious control and is thus left to chance.

INTERLUDE

Any piece of music played or sung between the movements of a larger composition.

ISORHYTHMIC

Pertaining to an isorhythm, a medieval principal of construction which was used most often in motets. This construction is based on a repeating rhythmic pattern in one or more of the voices.

Glossary

LARGAMENTE

It., a directive to perform a designated passage of a composition with a broad, full sound.

LINEAR HARMONY

Harmony that results from melodic motion without regard for traditional harmonic progression.

MAESTOSO

A directive to perform the designated passage of a composition in a stately, dignified, majestic fashion. It., majestic.

MAJOR

Term referring to a sequence of notes that define the tonality of the major scale. The tonic is followed by the next note a whole step up from the tonic; the third is a whole step from the second; the fourth is a half step from the third, the fifth is a whole step from the fourth; the sixth is a whole step from the fifth; the seventh is another whole step, followed by the tonic, a half step, above the seventh. Thus the first and eighth tones are exactly an octave apart.

MELODY

A tune; a succession of tones comprised of mode, rhythm, and pitches so arranged as to achieve musical shape, being perceived as a unity by the mind.

METER

Measure of time; arrangement of poetical feet; the grouping of beats into regular patterns. The organization of rhythmic patterns in a composition in such a way that a regular, repeating pulse of beats may continue throughout the composition.

MINOR

A series of tones that defines a minor tonality. The natural minor scale has the same tones as the major scale, but uses the sixth tone of the major scale as its tonic. Thus, the semitones (half steps) are between the second and third tones and the fifth and sixth tones.

MODAL

Having to do with modes; this term is applied most particularly to music that is based upon the Gregorian modes, rather than to music based upon the major, minor, or any other scale. Sometimes referred to as church modes.

Glossary

MODULATION

The process of changing from one key to another.

MOTIF

A short tune or musical figure that characterizes and unifies a composition. It can be of any length, but is usually only a few notes long. A motif can be a melodic, harmonic, or rhythmic pattern that is easily recognizable throughout the composition. Fr.

MISTERIOSO

A directive to perform a certain passage of a composition in a mysterious manner; mysteriously. It.

OBBLIGATO

It., obligatory. An accompanying, yet very important part of the music that that should not be omitted, such as a countermelody.

OCTAVE

An interval spanning seven diatonic degrees, eleven semitones. An octave above C would be C.

OFFERTORIUM

A composition performed during the collection of the offering in the Mass. The Offertory follows the Credo. May refer to spiritual offering musically expressed.

PARODY MASS

A Renaissance style of composition, especially prominent in the composition of Masses, in which older material was used in the creation of new music. For a composition to be a parody, it was necessary to incorporate the entire substance of the original material into the new, not merely a tune or a few lines of text.

PARALLELISM

Common literary feature of Hebrew poetry in the Old Testament in which words of two or more lines of text are directly related in some way. The use of parallelism usually means that the message of the text is in the larger passage. Parallelism can clarify ambiguity in word meanings.

PASSACAGLIA

It., a continuous variation form. The basis for the form is a four bar ostinato (A short pattern that is repeated throughout an entire composition). It is similar to the chaconne and is moderately slow in triple meter. It.

Glossary

PESANTE

It., a directive to a musician to perform a certain passage in a heavy, ponderous fashion, with importance and weight, impressively. It.

PIANO

Dynamic marking meaning quiet. A directive to a musician to perform a certain passage softly (abbreviated p).

PICARDY THIRD

The sudden shifting from the melancholy and sadness of the minor mode to the strength and assuredness of the major tonality.

PYTHAGOREAN THEOREM

The theorem that the square of the hypotenuse of a right triangle is equal to the sum of the squares of the other two sides. Musically speaking, this ratio is the basis for the major scale. The major scale is derived acoustically by Pythagoras from the perfect fifth.

QUASI UNA FANTASIA E BRILLIANTE

In the style of. . . ; in the manner of . . . ; somewhat. So... in the style of fantasia or rhapsody and with a brilliant and exciting mood. It.

RAISON D'ETRE

A reason to be. Fr.

RECAPITULATION

In sonata-allegro form, the recapitulation is the final presentation of the original theme group, first presented in the exposition. Usually the recapitulation is entirely in the tonic key of the composition. This is the third and main division of sonata-allegro form.

SEMPRE PIU ALLARGANDO

Always becoming broader, louder and slower (Literal translation). It.

STRETTO

In a fugue, that situation in which the subject and answer overlap one another, or when two subjects enter in close succession. Term sometimes used to indicate a quickening of tempo. It., pressed, closed.

STRING THEORY

A theory stating, simplistically, that the most fundamental particles of matter are, no more or less than, infinitesimal strings of vibrating energy

Glossary

TACET

An indication in the music that a performer is to be silent for some time. Typically, for an entire section or movement of a composition. Lat., he is silent.

TALEA

Term used in the Medieval era to denote a freely-invented rhythmic pattern. Lat.

TARANTELLA

A dance in fast 6/8 time having a delirious, mad character to it. The tarantella is characterized by alternations between major and minor tonalities and a quickening of speed throughout the composition. It was thought to cure any dancer from deadly spider bites.

TEMPO

The speed of the rhythm of a composition. Tempo is measured according to beats per minute. It., time.

THEME

The musical basis upon which a composition is built. Usually a theme consists of a recognizable melody or a characteristic rhythmic pattern. The theme may sometimes be called the subject.

TONAL

Term referring to music that is based upon major and minor tonalities rather than on modal, twelve-tone, or other musical systems. Tonal and Real: In a fugue, if the answer has exactly the same intervals as the subject, the only difference being that it is transposed, the answer is said to be real. If the answer varies from the subject it is said to be tonal.

TRANSITION

Passing out of one key into another; also, a passage that takes the composition from one key into another.

VESPERS

The seventh service of the Divine Office, usually performed at twilight. The service consists of several responsories and psalms which are sung. Lat., evening.

VOCA ME CUM BENEDICTUS

Lat., count me as blessed

About the Author

etti Harris is retired from a long and colorful career as a teacher both of music and aviation. She received her early musical education from private teachers at the military academy at West Point, New York, but it was later in life when, at age forty, she began her formal training at Westminster Choir College and Montclair State University in New Jersey to become a degreed teacher. During her years at Westminster she sang in the renowned Westminster Choir, singing in many well-known concert halls and serving as a member of the choir in residence at the Spoleto, Italy, Festival of Two Worlds. She became a licensed FAA instructor pilot in 1981.

Throughout her myriad experiences as teacher and performer, Harris maintained an active pursuit of what she called "truth in music" which embraces not only her fervent faith in God, but also the raison d'etre of music as an integral part of our entire human experience.

Harris now lives with her husband in Forest, Virginia, where she is actively pursuing her research and writing.

CPSIA information can be obtained at www.ICGtesting.com
Printed in the USA
BVOW041611220911

271867BV00001B/8/P